NO FIXED ADDRESS

A FOUR-YEAR-OLD'S JOURNEY FROM PILLAR TO POST DURING WWII

DAVID A. WILLSON

No Fixed Address
A Four-Year-Old's Journey
from Pillar to Post During WWII

REMF Books, Maple Valley, WA
Copyright © 2016 David A. Willson
All rights reserved.

ISBN-10: 0-692781-76-5
ISBN-13: 978-0-69278-176-0

DESIGNED BY KRAMER O'NEILL

PRAISE FOR *NO FIXED ADDRESS:*

David Willson has done it again. *No Fixed Address* is a delightful read. With his gentle wit and the emotional honesty we expect from him, David tells a deceptively simple story using the graceful prose of a writer who knows exactly what he is doing. The characters are complex, human, funny, some of them mean, and David's writing makes me wish I could have met every one of them. In the fine tradition of Tony Earley and Homer Hickam, this book touches you on every page.

> —Patrick Sheane Duncan, Writer, Director, Producer,
> Veteran, book-ophile

No Fixed Address is a brilliant collection of short stories written by a master storyteller. This work is insightful, heartwarming, and honest. David Willson manages to weave a complex relationship between a mother and a son through the fluidity of the past with the present, and through a son's alternating point of view—child and adult and child. This convention makes *No Fixed Address* beautifully deceptive in its simplicity. Mr. Willson is a great writer who should be read — and studied.

> —D.S. Lliteras, author of *Viet Man* and *Flames and Smoke Visible*

I've been a huge fan of David Willson's work since I was bowled over by *REMF Diary*, his hilarious, semi-autobiographical Vietnam War novel. In his new, compulsively readable collection, David shows off his dry wit and his brilliant story-telling ability as he shines an illuminating light on a unique and little-remarked time and place: the home front during World War II. Highly recommended.

> —Marc Leepson, Arts Editor, The VVA Veteran and editor of
> *The Webster's New World Dictionary of the Vietnam War*

I first encountered David Willson's drily rapier wit when he delivered a talk at a conference on the Vietnam War in Manchester, England, back in 1986. That same quirky sense of humor, coupled with his keen ability to observe what goes on around him, is evident in *REMF Diary* and subsequent books based on his military service. I was expecting more of the same in *No Fixed Address*. Instead, I've found the reminiscence of a melancholy young boy struggling to cope with the impact of World War II on his family and himself. This is a sweet story, a lovely story, deeply affecting, a window into American history that is uniquely Willson's.

— W. D. Ehrhart, American poet, memoirist and essayist

Homer is a railroad man back from his war in the Philippines. His dad came back from the Civil War. His son is at Iwo Jima. Grandson Davy, four years old, lives with his mom and the old man in his boxcar. Readers of David A. Willson will know that the small boy is on his own way to Long Binh, United States Military Assistance Command, Republic of Viet Nam, where we dumped Agent Orange into the water supply every day on our way back from each sortie. Attend to the swan song of the Rear Echelon Mother Fucker who is himself an old man now, the magician who has broken his wand of savage irony to tell as simply as possible the story of four generations of anger and war and the love and work that a stove-up grandfather could teach.

— Dan Duffy, Viet Nam Literature Project

NO FIXED ADDRESS

DAVID A. WILLSON

To Michele, my Angel of Mercy. Without her, nothing.

CONTENTS

POST, FOUR: THOMPSON FALLS

PILLAR, FIVE: BALLARD ONCE AGAIN

POST, SIX: AFTER THE WAR

PILLAR, ONE: BALLARD

INTRODUCTION:
A LETTER FROM NOVEMBER 1941

Yesterday, March 31, 2015, I got a packet in the mail from my sister, Leanne. There was a note, short and breezy, and a ream of paperwork to be filled out as part of the ordeal of retrieving our late mother's money from avaricious banks. Mother died not long ago, at 92, and my younger sister has been acting as her executor.

Also enclosed was a letter, written in November of 1941.

The letter is handwritten by both my father and my mother, Bob and Alice Willson, on both sides of a small piece of pretty good bond paper. At the top is their address of that date: 1413 West 64th Street, Seattle, Washington. It was written to my father's parents, Grandpa Homer and Grandma Katherine, who lived in Montana.

The text:

Dear Mom & Pop,

We haven't heard from our last letter yet but we thought we'd write anyway & tell you the news. Alice doesn't seem to know just how to tell you but anyway you're going to be grandparents. Hi Gram and Granpop! It isn't going to happen until July tho. Guess you know from that that Alice hasn't been feeling so hot lately. Of course we've been to a doctor and will keep going. He says she's the tough skinny type and ought to put on a little weight.

We're both really happy and glad we're going to have a baby but we don't know for sure yet what we'll name it. Do you 'spose it'll be a boy or a girl?

I hope you'll both be as happy as we are to know we're going to be parents.

Seeing as how Alice is kind of under the weather, Mom, maybe you'd better wait a little longer till she feels better before you come see us. We don't know just how much longer it'll be and we do want you to come but not till Alice feels more like herself.

Goodbye for now and let us know how it feels to be future grandparents. Lots of love.

Your son, Bob

++

Got your letter today & was glad to hear that everything is fine.

I've been feeling pretty punk lately but I guess that is to be expected. I hope I will soon stop feeling oozie in my tummy.

I wouldn't be very entertaining company feeling as I do, but hope you will come when I feel better.

Love, Alice

I wasn't born yet when my parents wrote this letter, and now both the letter writers are dead. The then-grandparents-to-be are long since dead, too.

This is a letter I've never seen before, and I'm stunned it survived my parents' relentless destruction of family memorabilia, especially old letters. I wish I knew why this one letter survived. Accident? Probably not.

We know the baby was a boy, and he wasn't born in July, but on June 3oth, and that they named him David. We know that stuff now.

INTRODUCTION

One week after this letter to Bob's parents, the Japanese bombed Pearl Harbor, and the whole game changed. After Pearl Harbor, nobody was very happy about having a baby. In fact, people who were having babies were considered to be bad planners. Once I was born, I became a problem to be worked around.

These simple stories are written from my memories of the late WWII era. From the point-of-view of the problem being worked around: a four-year-old boy whose father has become a Marine.

FROM PILLAR TO POST

My grandma Alma, my mom's mom, lived with Grandpa Hulver near us in Ballard on the corner of West 5oth Street, in a huge old house that she ran a boarding house in.

We didn't live in our own little house long, only until Father got his draft notice to go off and kill Japs, as everyone in the family put it. I was so young I have few memories of life in that house, and those I have are a mixture of my memories and the stories I was told by Mother and by Aunt Lee.

My mom told me I was a colicky baby who screamed and screamed after she nursed me. The only thing that calmed me and put me to sleep was for Father to take me on the sofa with him and hold me tight on his belly and rock me. That was a soothing image, but hard to imagine. After the war, Father would not abide noise, and he also did not abide the holding and comforting of Leanne, who was born in 1947 and had high needs for attention, all of which flowed from Mother.

My parents got rid of their little house when Father was drafted. Mother said that Father told her that it would be a burden for her, both to take care of and to pay for, so that was that. Gone. Mother expected to follow Father where the Marines sent him, so far as that was possible. She didn't want to stay in Seattle at the mercy of her mother. I was not sure what she meant by that, but Mom and her mother had always fought, and continued to do so. Mom was a fighter, and so was her mother.

So Mother followed Father to San Diego, California, where he was trained to be a Marine at Camp Pendleton. He'd wanted to be a Naval pilot, but the Navy told him they had a higher need for Marine Corps riflemen, so that is what he was trained to do. Uncle Roy was there at the same time, but he got rheumatic fever and ended up in the Naval Hospital. His wife, Lee, my mother's sister, was with us in San Diego to be near Roy.

The mood of that time was dark. As a kid, it seemed to me that both Uncle Roy and my father were expected to die. Uncle Roy from his fever, and my father at the hands of the Japs, who were winning the war in the Pacific.

I didn't miss the house in Ballard, but I did miss my father. I associated him with the house. Both were lost around the same time, forever. Mother and I saw little of Father in San Diego. I remember him in Balboa Park, right before he left for the Pacific. Perhaps what I remember are the photographs taken that day. And the peacock. I think the peacock is an honest memory of my own. Not one from a family story or based on a photo. But how can I be sure? I remember I went up to it and it squawked at me and scared me half to death. And everyone laughed. Not funny to me. I was often a figure of fun to the adults I was surrounded with. They had no other children to laugh at, just me, and they didn't seem to remember when they were kids. Being the only kid around wore on me.

I have an album with a half-dozen photos of the interior of the little house in Ballard, and a few more of the yard and the exterior of the house. Black and white photos, inexpertly taken, but valuable for the information they contain.

Because it was taken the day before Christmas, the photo that made the biggest impact on me is one of my mother, in the living room of the house, sitting all alone on a striped hassock in front of a sparsely-limbed and -needled fir tree. The photo is dated December 1941. It is obviously late December. The Japs had bombed Pearl Harbor, and my mother, who was born in 1922, was pregnant with me, about three months. Mother is not looking at the photographer, who was probably my father, but at the sad tree, decorated with some tinsel and a few lights and a few little ornaments. There are some presents under the tree. Mother's hands are crossed prayerfully in her lap, and her ankles are crossed. She looks very pensive.

Mother is wearing a dark dress with many buttons down the front of it, with white trim at the neck, maybe lace. Dark shoes. There's a tall candle on a nearby table. Her hair is pulled back austerely. Curtains are drawn. There is an old-fashioned oak crank telephone mounted on the nearby wall. Beneath it on the floor is a tall vase containing fir boughs. I think the vase is the Roseville vase I remember having a place of honor in our house in Yakima. By then, it had several large chips in it. There is a nice carpet on the wooden floor. An old oak library table is near the telephone. The striped sofa is under the front window, right next to the door. It has one ornamental pillow on it.

I was born June 3oth, 1942. My father was inducted into the Marine Corps on June 26th, 1944. He served until April 3, 1946. His Marine Corps service number was 978955. He had worked at Boeing as an expediter until inducted.

The stories in this book take place during that period, twenty-one months. Mother and I were knocking around on our own, with Aunt Lee, or we were camped out with Grandpa and Grandma Aspen in Ballard in their basement, or with Grandpa and Grandma Willson, Father's parents, in Thompson Falls, Montana. I was happy in both places, as I could spend time with my grandfathers. I was their only grandchild. The most grandchildren the Willsons ever had was four, and I was the first. My sister always was troubled that I had a five-year head start on her. I always felt that I shouldn't be blamed. I never asked to be brought into this world. All my baby and childhood pictures show I was not happy about it. What was there to be happy about? Not much.

The other photos of the little house in Ballard reminded me of one thing I had been happy about. I had a red wagon that had the words "Bull Dog" printed on the sides. It showed an artistic representation of a bulldog, and my father is pulling me along in the wagon. Or at least pretending to for the photo. I'm sure I wanted that wagon because it had a bulldog pictured on it. I was mad about dogs. I loved them and I wanted one. But I could not have one until the war was over. So I was told, over and over again. So I got a Bull Dog wagon instead. That had to do. Meanwhile, I latched onto every dog that wandered close. I was warned, but I didn't care. There are many pictures of me as a toddler with one dog or another.

On Christmas, 2014, I called my ninety-two-year-old mother to talk to her, as I did every day. Our conversations of late had been vague and not at all normal, due to Mother's ill health, so I hoped that having an ancient subject close to her heart might bestir her to come up with some information, and perhaps cause her to become a bit more animated. So we discussed that photo of her in that little house in Ballard, taken seventy-three years ago, before I appeared on the scene.

"That was a nice house," she said. "It had an upstairs with one big room. That was your room. We slept downstairs."

"How did that work?" I asked.

"It worked fine. You cried a lot. We couldn't hear you so much," she said.

Okay. That explained a lot.

"You were colicky after you were nursed."

* * *

My mother had been in serious trouble with her health for a few weeks due to a couple of falls in quick succession. A month before, she'd informed me, "I want someone to take care of me. I'm ninety-two years old. I'm tired of taking care of myself. Doing everything for myself." Shortly after that announcement, she took a serious tumble in her bathroom chasing down a "big ugly bug." When I took her to task for doing that, she asked, "What was I supposed to do, let it go?"

"Sure, or call security," I said.

"I wanted to get it myself," she said.

"How did that work out for you?"

"Badly. Now I am in a lot of pain. And in the hospital," she said.

"But there are people taking care of you," I said.

"They are very slow. And not there when you need them," she said. "I need Leanne or Sally to be here."

A few days after she hairline-fractured her pelvis going after that big ugly bug, she fractured a vertebra. No big ugly bug involved this time. Just a toilet seat she sat down on much too hard. A new toilet seat had been installed to make things easier for her. It was about three inches taller than the old one. So Mom sat down hard, as though the seat were much lower. And…pain. A fractured vertebra, just that fast. Old bones.

When I discussed that incident on the phone with my sister Leanne, she said Mom's subconscious mind dictated these two events, as "she wanted to be taken care of."

I said, "Mom does not believe in such a thing. To her there is no subconscious mind."

"No, she doesn't believe in depression either, but she's been depressed most of her life," Leanne said.

"She thinks depressed people are just lazy and weak. If they kept busy, they wouldn't think they were depressed," I said.

"Yes, Mom has told me that many times. I just need to pull up my socks. To get a grip," she said.

"Mind over matter," I said.

"Something like that," she said.

In our Christmas phone conversation, Mom couldn't remember the details of selling the house and moving out when Dad was drafted.

"It was something he wanted to do. He didn't want me living in a house with you without his being there to take care of it," she said. "'The roof needs attention. I don't want you going up on that roof to fix those loose shingles,' he said. I told him I wouldn't. 'You are likely to do so if one of those shingles blows loose. I don't want to have that to worry about on top of the Japs. I'll need to keep my mind clear. We're selling the house,' he said. And that was that. I'd grown up in a family where Mom and Dad were always fighting. I didn't want a life like that. I wanted a life with no fighting, so I let your dad have his way about everything. That way there was no fighting."

"Are you happy now that you took that path?"

"Well, no, your father had really bad judgment about a lot of things and made a lot of really bad decisions, especially about money. On his death bed, he told me he wished he'd taken my advice more than he did," she said.

"Like about not investing in that dairy farm he lost all that money on," I said.

"Yes, or that acre of land in Texas," Mom said. "He thought there'd be oil on it. He always invested with 'Good Christian men wearing dark suits and white shirts and ties. They are good Christian men,' he'd always say. As if he could see into their hearts. And I'd say, 'They are conmen,' and he'd get really mad at me. And our money was gone."

"So we didn't have our little house in Ballard during the war?"

"No, you and I were dashed from pillar to post, staying in tourist cabins, cheap hotels, peoples' basements, and in boxcars. No fixed address. That's how your father wanted it. No roof for me to climb and fall off of. We moved constantly while your father was in the Marines."

She added, "You've heard the stories from me and Aunt Lee,"

"Yes, I've heard the stories," I said.

AUNT ALLIE VISITS THE BALLARD HOUSE

One of the World War II stories that I'd heard most often from my mother, while I was growing up, was the one about the time that Aunt Allie and Uncle Bruce came to visit us from Trout Creek, Montana. Aunt Allie's professed reason to visit was to see "Bobby"— that's my father—before he'd gone to be a soldier, or in his case, to be a Marine. To kill Japs.

I suspect the real reason was that she wanted to come to Seattle to shop. One of the great joys in her life was to shop for hats. Spokane held few joys for her, shopping-wise—Spokane being the big town that Western Montanans drove to for serious shopping. Spokane wasn't much better than Missoula, as far as Aunt Allie was concerned, at least not for finding a remarkable and stylish hat.

Though I figure that Aunt Allie did want to see my dad. She and Uncle Bruce had no children. Aunt Allie was actually my great-aunt, Father's mother's aunt.

My grandparents had had a daughter, Marjorie, who died of Spanish influenza in January of 1919 at the age of two. My father was born December 27th, 1919. He was both treasured and kept at a distance by his parents after Marjorie's death. Aunt Allie was always close to him. And so she made the trek from Trout Creek, Montana, to Ballard, in Seattle, Washington.

I have an old family album that contains many, many photos of Aunt Allie in her full glory. She loved to have her picture taken, and she posed as though she were a raving beauty. She was a tall woman, taller than Uncle Bruce, who was a little man, and she was large of build, with a very plain face—no smile ever. In one of my favorite pictures, she's standing next to a car circa 1915, and she looks almost as large as the car.

Aunt Allie and Uncle Bruce rode the train to Seattle, and my father picked them up at the depot downtown and brought them to our house in Ballard. They stayed with us for one week. Father was still working at Boeing, finishing up his expediter job. What that entailed, I still have no idea.

"That week seemed like an eternity to me," my mother told me many years later. "Aunt Allie thought she was a princess. She sat down in the easy chair in the corner of our living room when she arrived, and never lifted a finger to help herself. She barked orders at me the whole week."

Aunt Allie would trill, "Alice," in her high-pitched babydoll voice, and expect Mother to be at her beck and call, to produce whatever Aunt Allie needed at that moment. Uncle Bruce was usually out in the backyard smoking, or he would walk over to the Ballard taverns with one of my great uncles to drink beer until all hours. He'd come home "three sheets to the wind," according to my mother.

Mother was left with the job of entertaining Aunt Allie. Aunt Allie was too fat to walk anywhere, like the three blocks to Grandma Aspen's boarding house, so my mother was stuck. "I think I served her three hundred cups of tea, and she'd only drink from English bone china. She never washed a single teacup or saucer. She had to have fresh baked cookies with her tea. Covered with a little warm doily. I think I lost ten pounds during that week," Mom said. "Aunt Allie got fatter."

The big event that week was a dinner that Grandma Aspen had in Aunt Allie's and Uncle Bruce's honor, as guests from Montana, which was thought of as the Wild West. The joke was that Aunt Allie was way more la-di-dah than Grandma Aspen, who was pretty matter-of-fact about manners and customs.

But also, the dinner was a farewell to my father before he left for Marine Corps boot camp.

Where Aunt Allie got her pretensions, I didn't know. My Aunt Nellie Mae told me, some time ago, that the family take on Aunt Allie was that she'd worked in a Butte, Montana, house of ill fame. When I asked her what Aunt Allie's draw would be in a Butte whorehouse, she said there were two things: her considerable bulk was attractive to many of those lusty miners, and she had a physical oddity.

I pressed Nellie Mae for details on this.

"Aunt Allie had a third breast," she said.

My jaw dropped a mile, and I stared at her.

"I saw it," Nellie Mae said. "I saw all three of them, at the same time."

I didn't ask her how that happened. She added, "And there's a third reason, that you know about."

"What's that?"

"Why, she provided a gateway to the spirit world. You're the one who inherited her crystal ball and her book of Emmanuel Swedenborg's Heavenly Arcana. Aunt Allie was a medium, and said to be a good one."

"Really?"

"Men thought so. You know how gullible men are."

"Yes, I do. If any man does, I'm that man—Mr. Gullible," I said. "I always enjoyed Aunt Allie, but she died when I was so young, I'm no judge of what men might have seen in her, or what Uncle Bruce saw in her."

"He adored her," Nellie Mae said. "He couldn't keep his little hands off of her."

"I do remember that game they played. Where he'd sit in her chair. She'd come into the room and sort of prance over to him, sit on his lap and then look around and ask, 'Where's Brucie?' That made me laugh as a young kid," I said

"It was funny the first couple of times, but I got sick of it," Nellie Mae said. "But your grandma always had a great fondness for her Aunt Allie. Bob never really took to her, but Aunt Allie was oblivious to that."

So we had that big dinner at Grandma Aspen's, before my dad left for the Marines. I remember nothing about that night, but I've been told about it so many times, I feel as though I do remember it. Memory and imagination are close cousins.

Mom told me that Aunt Allie wore her huge beaver fur coat that made her look like a grizzly bear. It was raining hard the night of the dinner, so she got mighty wet walking from the car to Grandma's house from the curb. Uncle Ludwig, who was there, said that not only did Aunt Allie look as big as a grizzly bear, but she also smelled like one, due to that wet fur.

Aunt Allie not only wore the fur coat, but she also wore a new hat she had bought in a little shop in Ballard. Mom told me that it was made from the feathers of at least three Chinese pheasants. Father, the bird hunter in the family, made that pronouncement, she'd said.

As Uncle Ludwig described it, "Aunt Allie came through the front door of Grandma Aspen's house like the Great Ship Titanic trying to pass through the Homer Chittenden Locks in Ballard." Uncle Lud had been assigned the role of butler that night by his mother. Mom says that Aunt Allie knocked over two table lamps and one end table, before Uncle Lud wrestled her coat and hat away from her. Mom said that he was laughing so hard she feared for his health. He told her he'd rather wrestle an alligator.

* * *

Dinner was Grandma Aspen's famous beef pot roast, with roasted whole potatoes, onions, carrots and rutabagas, all of it drowned in a thick brown gravy. Also, Grandma's home-baked dinner rolls, each of which was as large as a baby's head. Lingonberries were served in a large dish with a big spoon stuck in it.

Grandma's food was always delicious and plentiful, but because Aunt Allie was served first, all the slices of pot roast with any fat on them were gone when she passed the platter on. Uncle Bruce was served next, but he "ate like a little sparrow," according to my mother. By the time the food got to my father, all the beef was gone and most of the vegetables, and all of the gravy.

Grandma swept up the empty platters and the gravy boat, and went off to the kitchen, where she replenished them. She'd cooked enough for an Army company, as usual, so there was no problem.

Father loved Grandma Aspen's cooking as much as he despised his own mother's. "Great dinner, Ma," he told her, as he always did.

Uncle Lud's fiancée, Florence, was there, but Mom says she never said a word. Mom says there was no discussion, not even a mention, that my father was going off to the Marine Corps soon.

Bruce said little or nothing. Aunt Allie talked about her new hat—the one made out of three Chinese pheasants, birds that my father called "chinks." Aunt Allie did not let a constantly full mouth deter her nonstop narrative about hat shopping.

My mother said, "Your Uncle Lud always was a great tease. So he asked her about her hat. 'Mrs. Babcock, how did you pick out that new hat of all the other hats in the Ballard Ladies' Hat Shoppe? How could you choose from so many beautiful hats?'

"'It was easy,' she said in that little-girl voice of hers. 'I love feathers. I chose the one with the most feathers. I just love feathers.'

"'Don't leave your house during bird hunting season back in Montana, Mrs. Babcock,' Lud advised.

"Aunt Allie laughed around a mouthful of one of Grandma's dinner rolls, slathered with butter and lingonberries. 'Aren't you a sweet boy, to think I might be mistaken for a Chinese pheasant? You are a funny boy, Ludwig. And a cute boy, too.' And she pinched Lud's cheek. Lud didn't tease Aunt Allie any more after that. But Aunt Allie was right. Lud was a cute boy and a funny boy. Why he married that dull Florence is beyond me. Well, I do know why. She was Ma's pick. Lud was crazy about an Italian Catholic girl who was a cheerleader. Your grandma put the kibosh on that. What a meddler she was. She didn't like my marrying your father. I just wanted to get out of that house and get away from Ma."

After Grandpa ate, he excused himself to seek out his bottle of wine he hid in the basement. Grandma was pleased that the two guests of honor, my great-aunt Allie and my father, had seconds and thirds of her food.

The next day, Dad drove Aunt Allie and Uncle Bruce back to the train depot to catch their train back to Montana.

"I was never so glad to see people leave my house, as Aunt Allie and Uncle Bruce," my mother said. "They both gave me the creeps. They were sleeping in our own bed, as it was the only bed big enough to contain both of them. I wanted to burn the sheets they used, but your father wouldn't hear of that. 'Waste not, want not,' he said. But the bed sagged from then on. When we sold the house, I was glad to include that broken bed as a bonus. I hated sleeping in that bed after it had been despoiled by those two. They were icky," Mom said.

I had to take her word for that. I was a kid. What did I know?

When I asked Mom if Aunt Allie had introduced her to the Angels of the Spirit World, she said, "You got to be kidding me."

I didn't broach the subject of the Butte, Montana, house of ill fame or Aunt Allie's third breast.

POST, TWO: NO FIXED ADDRESS

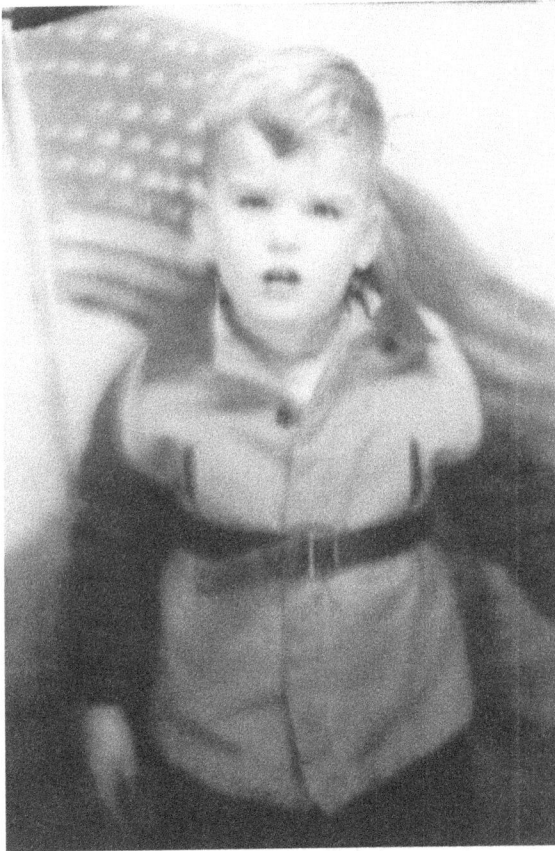

BALBOA PARK

When we went to visit Uncle Roy in the Naval Hospital in San Diego, I did not go in to see him. He was confined in a fever ward. For a long while, even Aunt Lee wasn't allowed to see him. He'd caught rheumatic fever during his Naval basic training and he wasn't the only sailor in training who got it.

I was told that those who got it and didn't die considered themselves lucky. Not because they didn't die, but because they were no longer headed to the South Pacific to kill Japs, and to perhaps be killed by Japs. The men with fever were done with war. Contrary to what we've been told by Tom Brokaw about the Greatest Generation—their eagerness to don uniforms, carry rifles, and march off to distant points to make the world safe for democracy—many were happy to not have to go. Happy to stay home and serve their country by doing black market deals on tires and gas, or busy themselves working at Hanford, producing the stuff that made Atomic bombs go boom. At that time this was all beyond me.

All I knew was that I waited with my mother in Balboa Park while Lee went into the huge hospital to visit Roy. Mom would try to keep me occupied while Lee was gone. Occasionally, Lee watched me while Mom went in to see Roy.

I loved Balboa Park because it was different from any landscape I'd ever seen before. It was like a foreign country to me. A foreign country with palm trees. There were no palm trees in Seattle or Thompson Falls, not that I'd ever seen. Some of the palm trees were tipped to look like huge fans.

And there were peacocks wandering around the park, on their own. I thought they were the most wondrous, exotic creatures on the planet. They entranced me. I'd been admonished by Mom and Aunt Lee again and again to stay away from them, that the birds could and would do me serious damage if I got too close to even one of them. But they were so beautiful and also silly-looking that I did not take the warnings to heart.

So one day, Mom and Aunt Lee and I were eating a picnic lunch on one of the park benches — a bunch of bologna sandwiches with no mustard, and a banana — when Mom and Lee got into one of their deep conversations. I wandered away and found a peacock to commune with. He was bigger than me, but I marched up to him. I wanted one of his feathers for my collection, and I thought I saw one that looked loose, ready to fall to the ground. I'd just help it along a bit, with a quick little pull.

"This won't hurt you, Peacock," I told him in my quiet voice. I reached out, got my fingers on the feather, and jerked it loose. He had allowed me to slowly and carefully approach him, but when I jerked on the feather, he shot up into the air and let out a squawk that caused me to tumble over backward into a rose bush.

The peacock landed on the ground and took off running away from me. I looked at my hand. I had the feather and it was a nice one. It had been attached to the big bird more firmly than I'd thought it was. I looked up as I saw tall shadows around me. I was surrounded by Mom and Aunt Lee.

"We can't take our eyes off you for one minute," Mom said.

"You are a bad little boy, to torment that bird so," Aunt Lee said.

"I just wanted this feather," I said.

"That feather was the bird's feather, not your feather," Mom said.

"I wanted it for my collection. He has so many. I didn't think he'd miss just one."

"You are a bad little boy," Aunt Lee insisted. "When I have my little boy, after the war, he won't do bad things like you do. He'll be a good little boy."

Little did she know that her little boy, Michael, would be so bad that he'd join a carnival; so bad that, at the height of the Vietnam War, he'd be rejected as unfit by the US Army.

"I'll give the feather back to the bird." I held up the feather.

"He won't want it back," Mom said. "You'd better behave yourself the rest of our time in the Park today, or you'll not be coming back."

Aunt Lee left us to go visit Uncle Roy in the hospital. Mother and I settled down on a bench in the sunshine to await her return. I played quietly with a little toy car I had in my pants pocket. I ran it up and down the side of the bench. My mother fell asleep on the bench. She always could fall asleep anywhere. I put my little car in my pocket and looked around for something to do.

I hopped off the bench and wandered down the sidewalk toward the hospital. There was a paved outdoor square area that drew my attention. There were men in blue bathrobes in wheel chairs, wheeling their chairs around and around in the sun. There was one man off to the side just sitting in his chair, reading a book. I walked up to him.

"Are you in the Navy, Mister?" I asked him. "My Uncle Roy is in the hospital with a fever."

He looked up from his book, startled at my question. "Where's your mother, little boy?"

"She's over there, asleep on the bench." I pointed.

"Well, I guess that's okay. We'll let her sleep. She probably needs her rest," he said. "Taking care of you is hard work."

"I guess so," I said.

"No, I'm not in the Navy. Not exactly. I'm a Marine."

"Like my daddy," I said.

"Your father is a Marine?"

"Yes, sir. He's gone to kill Japs."

"Let's call them Japanese," he said. "My name is Mac. What's your name?"

"My name is Davy. What happened to your legs?"

"My legs got blown off," Mac said.

"Did that hurt?"

"Not at the time. But later it did hurt. They hurt right now."

"But they're gone," I said.

"But the legs don't know that. That's the hell of it. They're gone, but they still hurt," Mac said.

"That's not fair."

"Very little in life is fair, Davy."

"What were you doing when your legs got blown off?"

"I was running on the beach with other Marines. The Marine on either side of me died. I was spared," Mac said.

"Spared?"

"Yes, I only lost both legs. I woke up days later on a hospital ship. The next thing I knew, I was here in San Diego in this hospital. My war was over."

"What did you do before the war?"

"I was a high school teacher and a basketball coach."

"This could happen to my dad."

"Where is he serving?"

"Guam," I said.

"Pray it doesn't happen," Mac said.

"Will that help?"

"I don't know, Davy."

"What are you reading?" I could see a picture of a dog on the cover of his book. "Is it a dog book?"

"Sort of. *Call of the Wild*, by Jack London,"

"My favorite book is *Poky Little Puppy*," I said.

"I like that one, too. I've read it to my little boy."

"What's his name?"

"Sammy," Mac said.

"Does he come to visit you?"

"He lives with his mother in New York, on the other side of the country. His mother doesn't want him to see me like this." He patted his empty pajama legs. "He's a sensitive boy."

"My mom says I am a sensitive boy," I said.

"I'm sure you are, Davy." He turned his head away from me. The sun caught his blond hair and made it look like it was on fire. He seemed very sad.

I patted his arm. "I like talking to you. I hope my daddy makes it home from the Marines. I'll love him whether he has legs or not."

Mac didn't answer me right away. "I'm sure you will, Davy," he said at last. "I hope your dad makes it back home in one piece."

"Will they let you teach school even though you are in a wheel chair?"

"It remains to be seen," Mac said.

"I hope they will."

"People in this country don't like cripples around," he said. "Even crippled veterans."

"Cripples?"

"People like me. People with missing limbs."

"But you were gone killing Japs," I said.

"Let's don't call them that. Let's call them Japanese."

"Why?"

"Because it's the right thing to do."

"Okay," I said.

"Your mother might be worried about you," Mac said.

"I pulled this feather out of a peacock." I held up the feather for him to admire.

Mac laughed. "I'll bet he loved that."

"No, he didn't. He let out a squawk."

"I'll bet he did." There were tears in his eyes. "I wish I'd seen that. That would have been something to see. You are a brave little boy."

"I am?"

"Yes, you are. Don't let anyone ever tell you anything different."

"Okay," I said.

"You'd better scoot back to your mother. It's been nice talking with you." Mac saluted me.

I saluted him back. Then I walked back around the corner to my mother. She was still sleeping on the bench.

PUNCHBOARDS

When I was not quite four years old, I was with my mother in a roadside diner, sitting on stools at the counter. There were punch-boards arranged along the counter. They were colorful and had nifty illustrations on them, mostly of pretty ladies who were struggling with their clothing. There was a nail provided. I picked out one of the boards and sat quietly, punching in the holes. Each punch I made caused a little pop, which my mother didn't notice.

But the counterman noticed. He got very angry and confronted Mom. "You owe me a lot of money, Lady."

"Why should I have to pay?" Mom asked.

"He's your kid, isn't he?"

"Yes, he is."

"Then you pay. Or you wash dishes."

"You shouldn't have those things sitting where a kid can get to them. It's like a trap," Mom said.

"You should have stopped him," the angry man said.

"I didn't notice, and I don't even know what those things are."

"What planet are you from, Lady?"

"What?" my mom said.

The ways of the world were mostly something she wasn't aware of or didn't know how to make sense out of. I knew that, even at that age. My Aunt Lee spent a lot of time explaining things to my mom, her baby sister.

We were there because my mother and I had gotten tired of walking. It seemed we'd walked for many dusty miles. It was just her and me. Usually, it was Aunt Lee and Mom and me, but Aunt Lee was at the Navy Hospital sitting at the side of Uncle Roy's bed. He'd gotten a fever and was slowly dying in the hospital. At least it seemed that way to me.

To tell the truth, I was the one who'd gotten tired. My mother could walk forever, but walking hurt my feet. Mother tried to carry me, but she was a tiny woman, hardly one hundred pounds, and I was a big kid, almost four years old. And a heavy kid. A chunk, they called me. My dad was nowhere around, so he couldn't carry me. He was gone to war to kill Japs with the Marines. At least that's what I'd overheard my grandpa say to my other aunt, my dad's sister. They didn't seem hopeful he'd make it back alive.

Mom and Aunt Lee and I had been evicted from another cabin, and Mom and I were trying to find a place that would rent to us. Nobody wanted to rent to a woman without a man, and if she had a kid, that made it almost impossible to find a place.

All the small dusty towns around Camp Pendleton had strings of roadside cabins to rent by the week, but mostly they were full, or not renting to young women with kids. I'd really liked the cabin we'd just left behind. There was a corner I liked to sit in and watch the spiders spin and crawl around. My mom and Aunt Lee liked that too, as I was out of their hair.

It took them a few days to figure out what I was doing in the corner. They'd not noticed the spiders. Aunt Lee was the one who noticed. She grabbed me up and put me on the saggy bed. Then she took a shoe and killed all the spiders. Thump, thump, thump. All my little friends were smashed. Then I was sad. I asked Aunt Lee, and she said, "Black Widow spiders. You're lucky you didn't get bit and die." Aunt Lee always saw the dark side of things. My mother would never have noticed. Stuff like that always passed her by.

But soon after that, the man from the cabin office tacked a piece of paper to our door, and we packed up our two little suitcases and walked up the highway to find another cabin. Aunt Lee took the bus to the Navy Hospital. She took her blue suitcase with her. Mom carried our brown-and-white-striped suitcase.

I'd gotten tired, dusty and thirsty after we'd walked a few miles. Also, my feet really hurt. I didn't whine, but I did say that I was thirsty.

"We'll stop just around the next bend," Mom said. She always said that. The joke was that we were walking along the side of a dusty concrete highway that was as straight as a yardstick. There were no bends, and there were no sidewalks. There wasn't much shade, either. And no place to sit down. There was a lot of litter, paper bags blowing in the wind and smashed beer bottles, and we saw one dead dog.

That made me sad, as I loved dogs. I'd never been lucky enough to own a dog, but Mom told me that after the war, she'd make sure I had my own dog. My favorite book was *The Poky Little Puppy*, and Mom had read it to me so many times that I had it memorized. Sometimes Mom tried to skip a page to get to the end faster, so she could tuck me into bed for the night, but I always knew. Sometimes I let her get away with it, because I knew that taking care of me really tired her out. It seemed to me that I was the only kid for a million miles.

There never was another kid to play with in any of the roadside cabins we stayed in. Occasionally, there was a crying baby somebody had smuggled in under a coat, but they were gone in a day. As I heard my Aunt Lee say to Mom, "Kids are a drug on the market." I also heard her say that she was glad she had waited to have a kid "after the war."

To me, it seemed there was no before or after to the war. It was all I remembered. I couldn't read the newspapers, of course, but I could tell that, when there were big dark headlines, people got very quiet. There were scary pictures of buildings burning, too, from bombs, I think. So I began to think the war would last forever. More than once I heard Lee say to Mom, "Bob might not come back from the Pacific. You have to prepare for that." Also, I heard Lee say, "I'm glad Roy is in the Navy Hospital. At least we know where he is."

The dog I wanted had to be a brown-and-white spotted one, like the *Poky Little Puppy*. Maybe a Cocker Spaniel, because Mom said I couldn't have a big dog. Cocker Spaniels were small but spunky. I could hardly wait for the war to end so I could have a dog. I brought it up so often that Mom and Aunt Lee had told me to "put a sock in it." I was encouraged to be very quiet, because the sound of a kid's voice alarmed or displeased most of the grown-ups we ran into. Often someone would say, "Can't you shut that brat up?" More than once, Mom or Aunt Lee were asked, "Don't you get sick of carting that brat around?" I understood that that brat was me.

"Don't you have grandparents you could park him with? You could have a lot more fun if that kid wasn't dragging you down." I did wonder why they brought me along. I would have been fine if I'd stayed in Thompson Falls with my dad's parents. But they both worked. Grandma was the telephone operator for the town, and Grandpa worked for the railroad. They had no time to take care of a kid. So I was carted around by my mom, like another suitcase.

Sometimes people would be nice to me and call me "Little Man." I didn't like that.

One sailor who'd taken an interest in my mom and my aunt went overboard with that. "So, Little Man, what's it like to keep company with two such pretty ladies?"

I didn't say anything.

"I'd really like to bunk in with the pretty ladies myself. You're a very lucky little man." Then he rubbed my head. I hated having my head rubbed. In fact, I hated being touched, especially by strangers. I backed off from him.

"If I give you a quarter, will you go play somewhere and leave us alone?"

"No," I said.

"You aren't very respectful to your elders."

"You're not my elder. You're nobody."

He smacked me when I said that. And then he was soon gone. There was a sort of an uproar. People didn't often hit me. He was the only stranger who ever hit me. Except for schoolteachers, who were still in my future. And they weren't really strangers. They mostly hit me because my handwriting was bad or because I was slow to catch on to things. That's okay, I guess.

My feet really hurt bad that day, and I did keep mentioning it. And Mom couldn't carry me and also tote that striped suitcase, so even though there never was a bend in the highway, we did stop at that roadside diner. Joe's Spot, it was called. It looked like a shiny train car. Mom ordered me a Coke, and water for her. We sat there a long time at the counter, resting with the suitcase by our feet. I'd gotten bored, and there were games sitting on the counter, with a nail to play them.

I took the one game with a pretty woman on it. Her legs were hanging out of her red dress, and her underwear was showing. Her top was pretty bare, too. Mom was sitting next to me, staring into space the way she often did. When I'd ask what she was doing—when I caught her attention, which wasn't easy—she'd say, "I'm thinking, Honey."

"About what?"

"Adult things." And that was all she'd say.

I punched a lot of holes in that game.

Later I learned it was called a punchboard. That made sense. And that each punch cost twenty-five cents.

The counterman was yelling at my mom about her having to wash dishes.

"Where's Joe? Are you Joe?" my mom asked.

"Joe? No, I'm not Joe," he said.

"Where's Joe?"

"He's gone. He's in the Army. In France."

"Why aren't you in the Army?"

"It's none of your damned business."

"You're afraid," she said.

"No, I have a hernia. The Army rejected me."

"A hernia?"

"Yes."

"Well," Mom said. "My husband is a Marine. He's killing Japs."

"Just pay for your Coke and get out of here. Don't come back with your brat," he said.

So Mom paid for my Coke.

She picked up our striped suitcase, and we left the diner. The door rang as it closed.

We resumed our dusty trudge up the side of the highway. "How will Aunt Lee find us?" I asked.

"We'll leave a message at the hospital," Mom said.

"Do we have a lot longer to walk?"

"Just around the next bend," Mom said.

NO FIXED ADDRESS

Mom and I trudged along the dusty highway for what seemed like forever.

I'm blank on how it happened, but we ended up in a hotel, not a roadside cabin. It was awful for me, as kids weren't allowed, so I had to not let out a peep. Also, there was no place for me to play. People were coming and going at all hours. We seemed to be the only people who stayed in our room all night long.

Lee met us at the hotel before we checked in, since no kids were allowed and she had to do the checking in for us. She was down, as Uncle Roy had "taken a turn for the worse," she said. He told her that at least he wasn't on a ship in the Pacific with suicide planes attacking day and night.

Mom said that Roy always looked on the bright side of things. "Just the opposite of Bob." Bob was my dad.

The hotel was very old and rickety. Lee checked us in, herself and Mom. I wasn't mentioned. Mom took me up to the second floor on the fire escape. The metal stairs rattled like they were going to pull loose from the rotten old wood of the building. Mom held my hand so tight that it went numb.

We sneaked down the musty hallway, which had a rug with stains and holes in it. We could hear activity in many of the rooms, rustling and banging and voices—high and low. And giggles. Lee had the door to our room open for us, and Mom shoved me in.

"Like two thieves in the night," Lee said. And it sort of was.

"You have to not let out a peep, or we're out on the street again," Mom told me.

The room was bare-bones. The one window had a tattered shade covering it, and no curtains. There was a big double bed, a dresser, and a very beat-up old sofa upholstered in big red flowers. "You'll sleep there." Mom pointed at the sofa.

It was better than I got sometimes. At least I had a place of my own to sleep.

As usual, I was hungry. Mom had bought a loaf of bread and a chunk of bologna. She hacked off some of it with a knife she'd taken from one of the diners we'd eaten in, and I sat on the sofa and ate it. It would have been better with some mustard. I said so.

"Kids don't like mustard," Lee said.

"I do," I said.

"Don't sass," Mom said. That was our usual exchange. Sassing was whenever I expressed my opinion.

I slept on the sofa that night with my usual blanket, Mom's and Lee's coats, thrown over me. I slept good, tired out from all the walking. That's what Lee had said. "You'll sleep good tonight after all the walking you did today."

The next morning, I had another bologna sandwich for my breakfast. I didn't mention the mustard. I washed down the sandwich with a glass of water from the bathroom. I would have liked milk, but as Mother said, "It would sour. You don't like sour milk."

She was right about that. But I didn't much like drinking the bathroom water, either. It was warm and rusty and the glass didn't seem real clean. The bathroom was dirty and it smelled bad, too.

There were rust stains in the sink, and in the bathtub, which had animal feet on it. The toilet was so nasty I hated to even sit on it. It had a cracked, yellowed seat and it didn't flush well.

After I ate my breakfast, Mom told me she and Lee were going to have to both be gone for a couple of hours. This wasn't the first time they'd left me alone, but it always scared me when they did. I worried if I'd ever see them again.

"Be a good boy. Quiet as a mouse. I made you another bologna sandwich. You can eat it for a snack if you get hungry," she said.

"Where are you going?"

"We're going to the Navy Hospital to see your Uncle Roy," Mom said.

"Is he going to die?"

"We hope not," Mom said.

Aunt Lee looked teary, and she wasn't much for tears. So I figured things must be bad.

"We want you to just sit on the bed and read your little book," Mom said. She meant *Poky Little Puppy*.

"We won't be gone all that long," Lee said.

"Just be very quiet and don't answer the door if anybody knocks," Mom said.

"Will somebody knock? Who?" I hadn't thought of that. That was scary.

"We don't know, but there might be somebody. Just be quiet and don't answer the door. Can you do that for us?"

"I'll try," I said. "Can you buy me some mustard in a little jar while you are gone?"

"We'll see," Mom said.

That usually meant no. They got all gussied up, and they left. They both kissed me goodbye, which they rarely did. It was like they expected not to see me again. I got a wobbly feeling in the pit of my stomach. I'd be glad when they came back. If they did. I wouldn't be able to live long on that chunk of bologna and that loaf of stale bread.

I sat on the bed for a long time reading my book. There was no clock in the room. I couldn't tell time anyway. I ate my sandwich and washed it down with warm, rusty water in that dirty bathroom glass. It seemed like hours later, when there was a knock on the door. I'd just used the bathroom and flushed the toilet. I didn't answer the door or speak. Who could this be?

"I know you're in there," a woman's voice said. "I heard the toilet flush."

I said nothing.

"If you don't answer the door, I'll call the police," she said.

The police. Anything but that. The police in California were all ten feet tall. I'd seen them many times, smashing their billy clubs into the heads of drunk sailors when Mom and Lee were carting me in and out of bus stations. Police were the last people Mom and Lee would want getting their hands on me.

What to do?

"Open up right now, or the next thing you know, the police will knock your door down."

I hopped off the bed, carrying my book with me, and went to the door. I opened it up and looked up at the person who'd knocked.

"What have we here? A little man? You're not supposed to be here," she said. She was a very pretty lady, older than my mom and Lee, and she wore a lot of makeup—what Mom and Lee, both good Lutherans, called "war paint." Her hair was very blonde. Much blonder than my mother's hair. And she smelled good, almost too good.

"I'm not a little man. I'm a kid. I'm almost four." I held up four fingers to help her figure it out.

"Kids aren't allowed in this fleabag dive," she said.

"I know that. That's why Mom sneaked me up the fire escape."

"She's a smart lady, but she broke the rules."

"What's she supposed to do with me?"

"Good question, Kid, but not my problem," she said. "Maybe she should have thought about that before she hatched you."

"I'm not a bird. I'm a little kid."

"Of course, you are. Who said you were a bird? Do you have a mental problem?"

"My cousins say I'm slow."

"Can you read that book?" she asked.

"I have it memorized."

"Then you can't be too slow. I never did too good in school, myself," she said. "Aren't you gonna invite me in?"

"Come in."

She came in and shut the door. She sat on the bed. Then she stretched out, dug in her bathrobe pocket, and brought out a pack of Camel cigarettes and a paper book of matches with a pretty lady like herself pictured on it. I could tell they were Camels by the package. My Grandpa Homer smoked that kind. His "smokes," he called them.

"Fetch me that ashtray, would you, Kid? Please." She pointed at the dresser.

I went over to the dresser and got the ashtray and handed it to her. She balanced it on her tummy and lit her Camel and took a big drag on it, and then blew out smoke. "Don't ever start smoking, Kid."

"I won't," I said. "It's a dirty weed."

"Where did you learn that?"

"From my Grandpa."

"He's a smart man."

"Yes, he is."

She patted the bed next to her. "Come up here on the bed and keep me company. Standing there with that book, you make me nervous."

"Okay." I climbed up next to her. "You smell real good."

"I hear that a lot," she said. "From men."

"I'll bet. You are a very pretty lady."

"I predict you'll do very well with the ladies a few years from now."

"Thanks. What does that mean?"

"You'll find out in your own sweet time. You are a cute little boy."

"Thanks," I said.

"I like that cowlick you have in front." She reached out and brushed it back from my forehead with her free hand. "I wish I had a little boy like you."

"No, you don't," I said. "I'm nothing but trouble."

"Is that what they say?"

"They say it when they think I'm not listening."

"Well, these are troubled times." She took another big drag on her Camel. "Sad times."

"Yes," I said. "War."

"You know about that?"

"Everybody knows about that," I said. "What's your name?"

"Call me Maisie. That's close enough. Aunt Maisie."

"Maisie."

"Yes. Where's your daddy?"

"He's gone to war. He's a Marine. He's killing Japs."

"How do you know that?"

"I hear things when people think I don't. I play possum."

"Smart boy. You're not as slow as they think."

"I hope not. My cousins said I'd be put in a special school for retards."

"They said that?"

"They did," I said. "My cousin Dicky said that."

"They sound like mean little bastards, at least cousin Dicky."

"They're mean, all right," I said.

The door opened and Mom and Aunt Lee came into the room.

Aunt Maisie didn't bat an eye. She stayed on the bed with her long legs stretched out.

"Who are you?" Aunt Lee asked.

"She's Maisie," I said.

"I'm babysitting your little boy." She took another drag on her Camel. "I like him."

"Thanks," Mom said.

"We'll take over from here," Aunt Lee said.

"So, I'm dismissed. The next time you need to leave your kid, let me know, and I'll be happy to look out for him," she said. "I stay right next door."

"Thanks," Mom said.

Maisie got up from the bed, put out her Camel in the ashtray, put the ashtray on the dresser, pulled her bathrobe together, and pulled the cord tight. As she went through the door, she turned and winked at me. "See you later, Kid." She closed the door behind her.

"Do you need a bologna sandwich?" Mom asked.

"Sure," I said. "Did you buy some mustard?"

WE'RE MEXICANS

We left that fleabag hotel later that day. Lee and Mom had found us another cabin in a roadside bunch of cabins much closer to the Navy Hospital. We were the only white people in the place; all the others were Mexicans. Everybody. Mom said that Lee could pass for Mexican when she wanted to, as she was very dark in the summer. Grandma said that Lee's darkness was proof there was a Laplander in Grandpa Hulver's family woodpile. But Lee had the family's blue eyes. Some of the Mexicans in the other cabins did, too. I found that out when I played with them back behind the cabins, on the edge of a swampy pond.

Lee said it was a sewage sump, and it did smell like it was. We splashed around in it just the same.

I tanned pretty well, too, like Lee, and my dark brown hair and dark brown eyes helped me fit in. Not knowing one word of Spanish was a problem, but I picked it up pretty fast. Four years old is a good age to learn another language. About all I have left now is "Andelay, Andelay," and I might have picked that up from a Speedy Gonzales cartoon.

We stayed in that cabin for a few weeks, until the government men came with uniformed police and barking dogs, to put us all in trucks to send us back to Mexico. The problem for me was I'd not come from Mexico. I'd been to Tijuana with Mom and Lee once, but that was it.

The police surrounded us kids before we could run, and then tried to match us up with the adults responsible for us. I was kind of scared, but Angelita, a little girl who was my friend, assured me I'd be okay. "They won't take you. Your mom and aunt will rescue you. They are gringos. You can see it from a mile," she said. "You, though—they might think you are a Mexican."

When the government men showed up, Angelita and I were together in her cabin. I'd gone over there with my book, *The Poky Little Puppy*, and we were sitting on her bed, reading it, when the big men in uniforms burst in. They asked our names. They didn't like my answer at all. I thought they were going to hit me, but all they did was yell. They could yell really loud.

The Immigration people were frustrated by me. They tried to get me to speak Spanish. I said the few words I knew, but there were only three or four. Angelita kept telling them I didn't know any Spanish, and they kept telling her to shut up.

It was mean for them to call me a wetback, but they called Angelita that name, too. And she was an Angel, just like her name. She'd save a chicken tamale from her dinner for me to eat, which was good of her. I was sick of bologna sandwiches. I offered her one once, and she just laughed at the idea of it. She had a laugh that sounded like music. Her eyes were big, and browner than mine.

Her mom was nice, too. It was just the two of them. The rest of her family had been caught and sent back to Mexico weeks before. Angelita told me that she had been born in California, and had then moved back to Mexico with her family. That confused me, but none of this made any sense.

One of the government men told me, "You're going back to Mexico, Poncho," and no matter what I said, he called me Poncho.

Angelita told me that most Americans thought all Mexican boys were called Poncho. "They are mean, mean men, and stupid, too," she said. She was right.

"Where are my aunt and Mom?"

I found out soon that they, too, had been grabbed by the Immigration people. They had no papers—no passports, no birth certificates, not even drivers' licenses. They had no car to drive. No money to buy a car. No money to buy much of anything. Bologna and a loaf of bread. No money even for mustard. We were as poor as the Mexicans. Both my mother and Lee were born in Seattle, and I had been born there, too. But we had no proof.

It took a lot of phone calls to straighten out this mess.

Later, Mom said that one of the cops told her she should know better than to hang around with wetbacks.

She got really mad at that. "My dad was from Norway," she told the Immigration man.

"Yeah, but he didn't swim over. That would have been a long, cold swim."

"No, he didn't swim. He came over on a boat," she said.

"You should not consort with Mexicans, or you might get deported. Where did you get that kid? Is his father Mexican?"

"What if he was? I'm American. My son is American."

"It doesn't work that way, Lady."

"My boy's father is a Marine. He's off killing Japs while you are here terrifying women and children," she said.

Lee stayed silent throughout this confrontation. Mom was always the mouthy one. She always stood up for her rights, which had set her up for many beatings from her mother. Lee always said that my mother was born talking back, and that she never quit.

* * *

Eventually, Mom, Lee and I were released from custody. We took our little suitcases and found another place to live. I never saw Angelita again. When I asked my mother where Angelita and her mother went, she said that Angelita was headed back to Mexico along with all the other Mexicans.

When I asked my mother why they left Mexico in the first place, she said that they came here for work, that they wanted to make money. That there was no money to be made in Mexico.

"I didn't like being a Mexican, even for a few hours," Lee said. "Those government men were mean and they called me a liar. I asked them how many Mexicans could speak English like me. They just ignored me and focused on my suntan. I was getting really scared. The doctor at the Navy Hospital vouched for me. And I did dig up that military I.D. I used to get in and out of Camp Pendleton. Lucky I found that. Or we'd be in a truck on the way to Mexico."

"Really?" I asked.

"Maybe not," Mom said. "Even as dumb as they were, they could tell we didn't fit in with the others, and all of the Mexicans were quick to tell them that we were Americans."

"They are a lot smarter than those Immigration people," Lee said. "They all seemed like dopes to me."

Mom said the experience made her glad to be an American, but also ashamed.

Coming from Seattle, we didn't hear any Spanish being spoken or see Mexicans. "Too cold and rainy for them there," Lee said.

"Too far for them to walk, too," Mom said.

We'd heard mostly Norwegian and Swedish where we had lived in Ballard. Some English with what Mom called a "heavy brogue."

In Thompson Falls, where we'd visited my father's parents, it was all white people, and no Norwegian or Swedish was ever heard.

California was very different.

Lee said that hundreds of years ago, California was part of Mexico. But they weren't doing anything with it, so America took it over and found gold. The Mexicans had it for hundreds of years, but never discovered anything.

"I love their chicken tamales," I said.

"That's their big contribution to the world—the chicken tamale," Lee said.

"It's a lot better than bologna and bread. With no mustard," I said.

"How did you get to be so fussy?" Lee asked.

"I don't know."

"Where did you ever even taste mustard on bologna?" Mom asked.

"Grandpa Homer made me a sandwich like that. He had a big jar of bright yellow mustard. He said it was French."

"That figures," Lee said. "I knew nobody in Ballard had fed you bologna with mustard."

"It's good to get to the bottom of that," Mom said.

"I'm going to miss Angelita and her mother's tamales," I said.

"It's a good lesson to learn," Lee said. "Nothing good lasts."

"I've still got my *Poky Little Puppy* book."

"I'm surprised the government men didn't take it away from you," Lee said.

"They did try. They asked me who I'd stolen it from. I told them my dad gave it to me. And that he was a Marine killing Japs."

"What did they say to that?" Mom asked.

"They just laughed," I said. "They said, 'There ain't no Mexicans in this war. Not enough frijoles to feed them all.'"

We moved on, once we'd gotten out of what Lee called "the clutches of the government men."

I would miss having Angelita and the other little kids to play with. I was never in one place long enough to make real friends, and mostly there were no little kids around. This had been the most little kids I'd ever seen in one place. Their parents didn't wait until after the war to have kids; I wondered why, but I never asked.

I never played with a Mexican kid again, and the only tamales I ever got to eat came out of a can my mother bought at the grocery store.

They were better than no tamales, but not much.

JAPS

"Mom, I keep telling people that dad is in the Marine Corps killing Japs, but I don't even know what that is," I said. "What is it?"

"I don't really want to talk about that right now," Mom said.

"Well, I really want to know."

"You don't need to know now. You are a child."

"Are Japs like bugs of some kind? What are they?"

"Give it a rest, please."

Aunt Lee spoke up. "I'll talk to you about it, if you really need to know." Lee had been just sitting there at the kitchen table in our most recent tourist cabin, drinking a cup of coffee. I hadn't even noticed her. She was that quiet. She spent long periods just drinking coffee and staring at the wall. I guessed she was worried about Uncle Roy, who was in the Navy Hospital with a fever.

"Okay."

"Japs are people," Lee began.

"They're people? Nobody talks about them like they're people."

"Well, they did a very bad thing. They sneaked their planes into the sky over Pearl Harbor and bombed and machine-gunned Americans and killed thousands of us. During the Christmas Holidays. We'd done nothing to them, and they decided to start killing us."

"That's it in a nutshell," my mom said.

"Did you ever meet any Japs, or know any?" I asked.

Lee wrapped her hands around her coffee cup. "Sure. They were Japanese then. A family lived right on the same block as we did. We went to school with them in Ballard."

"You went to school with them? Weren't you scared of them?"

"No, not at all. They were nice people," Lee said.

"How did they get a hold of bombs and planes and attack and kill us?"

"Well, that family, the Yamamotos, didn't do that," Lee said.

"I'm confused. You said they did."

"I told you," Mom said, "You're a little kid and don't need to know this stuff."

"I want to understand."

"You'll never understand it," Mom said.

"Why?"

"Because it doesn't make any sense," she said.

"What happened to that family?"

"The Yamamotos," Lee said.

"The Yamamotos," I said.

"Well," Lee said, "soon after they bombed Pearl Harbor, they were rounded up in trucks and taken away."

"Like they do with the Mexicans here in California, and like they tried to do to us," I said.

"Yes, like that. Except they weren't sent to Japan. They were put in special camps, far from Seattle."

"For their own protection," Mom said.

"From what?"

"From mobs burning down their homes," Lee said.

"But they weren't the ones who attacked Pearl Harbor, you said."

"No, but their people did," Mom said. "People who looked just like them. They couldn't be trusted. The Yamamotos went from door to door in our neighborhood, trying to get us to sign a paper that said they were good neighbors. None of us would sign."

"Why not? Were they bad neighbors?"

"No, they were good neighbors," Lee said. "But we figured if we signed, we'd be the next ones shipped off to camps. We didn't want that to happen to us."

"Why would that happen to you?"

"Why not?" Mom said. "When they thought we were Mexicans, they were ready to truck us to Mexico."

"It's scary to live in America," I said.

"Well, if you haven't done anything wrong, you have nothing to fear," Mom said.

"What did the Yamamotos do wrong?"

"They were Japs. That was their sin," Lee said.

"Japanese," Mom said. "We used to call them that."

"Until they sneaked up on us and bombed us," Lee said. "They shouldn't have done that. Now we are going to wipe them out. If we can. That's what America does."

"Like we did with the Indians," Mom said. "When they kept sneaking up and massacring us."

"Are all Indians dead?"

"Mostly. There are very few left," Lee said. "When is the last time you saw an Indian?"

"In a movie. A cowboy movie."

"Those are actors. Not real Indians," Mom said.

"Did the Yamamotos have any little kids?"

"Yes, they had two or three little kids living in their house. Grand-children," Lee said.

"What happened to them?"

"They were taken away," Mom said. "All of them."

"Even the little kids? They couldn't bomb anybody."

"They had to stay with their parents," Mom said.

Lee said, "I'm sure that nothing bad happened to them."

"How can you be sure? Something bad could happen. Something bad could happen to me."

"We try to look out for you, the best we can," Mom said.

"I know, but I'll bet the Yamamotos said that to their kids, too."

"Probably they did," Lee said.

"And it did no good."

"There's a lesson in that," Lee said.

"What's that?" Mom asked.

"You can't count on anything in this life. Just death and taxes," Lee said.

"What's that mean?" I asked.

"It means we all die. We all pay taxes," Mom said. "This stuff is all way over your head. I tried to tell you that. You shouldn't be worried about anything except losing your 'Poky Puppy' book or playing in the dirt with your little tin cars."

"My little tin cars are with Grandma in Seattle. There was no room for them in our suitcase."

"No, there wasn't," Mom said. "You got to choose one favorite thing to take. You picked the Poky Puppy book."

"What did the Yamamoto kids get to take with them?"

"Not much. One little suitcase," Lee said. "I watched them being loaded up. We didn't leave our houses, but we watched through the shades. They had to leave their home and all the big stuff. All the furniture, their lawn mower, all that. The Yamamotos each had a little suitcase. That was about it."

"What happened then?"

"What do you mean?" Lee asked.

"Their stuff. What happened to it?"

"Well, people went over there and took everything they wanted and then people broke out all the windows with rocks. They would have burned down the house, but they were fearful the fire might spread. The next week, government people came and boarded up their house."

"What did they do that was bad?"

"Well, they personally didn't do anything," Lee said.

"But their people," Mom said, "the Japanese, bombed Pearl Harbor and went to war with us."

"But the Yamamotos didn't do that."

"No, they didn't. They were in Seattle, in Ballard just like us," Mom said.

"None of it makes sense to me."

"You're a four-year-old boy," Lee said. "You are a smart four-year-old, but you're a little kid and can't be expected to understand international relations."

"Is that what grownups call war?"

"Yes, they do that," Mom said.

"I don't get it. When we go back to Ballard after the war to live, will the Yamamotos be there?"

"Not if they know what's good for them," Lee said. "Nobody will want them there. Nobody will want them around, in the schools or anywhere. If they are smart, they'll all go back to Japan, where they belong."

"Well, there won't be much left of Japan after we win this war," Mom said. "We'll bomb it flat."

"Maybe there won't be, but that's where they belong." Lee took a sip of her coffee. "That's where people who look like them live. If they're smart, that's what they'll do—all of them."

"It'll be interesting to see what happens," Mom said.

"We've got a long wait," Lee said. "The Japs will never give up. They'll fight down to the last man. It'll take years. It'll seem like forever."

"I hope not. I'd like to see my daddy again."

"We all would," Mom said.

THE TRAIN TRIP

Mom and Lee had an argument about something, and it was decided that Mom and I would take the train back to Seattle, to stay in the basement of my grandmother's big house in Ballard that she ran as a boarding house. Lee would stay in California so she could visit Roy in the Navy Hospital.

My daddy met my mom in that boarding house. He and Ludwig, who was Mom's brother, both worked at Boeing. Dad was an expediter.

When I asked Dad what an expediter did, he said that he expedited.

Dad didn't like to answer questions or to talk much. Lee liked to say, "Bob is the silent type. They forgot the strong part." Whatever that meant. Lee made a lot of comments like that. When she did, Mom would say, "Another cryptic comment from Aleda." Aleda was Aunt Lee's real name, just like my Uncle Ludwig was always called Lud, except by his mother, who called him Ludwig.

I don't know what Uncle Lud did at Boeing, but he got to do it for the whole war, never putting on a uniform to go kill Japs or anybody else. Anyhow, Uncle Lud met Dad at work. Back then, Dad was looking for a place to room where they served good meals, so Uncle Lud took him home to Ballard, to the big boarding house on the corner of 5oth, where Grandma served great meals. She made the best biscuits and cinnamon rolls. Also, her meatloaf was good, with brown gravy.

Dad took a room there, and met my mother, Alice. She majored in music at the University of Washington, but she quit and married my father. They soon had me, and Mother never went back to college.

Then Dad got drafted into the Marines, and we moved to California to be near Camp Pendleton where he got his training. Aunt Lee moved with us, to be near Uncle Roy as he went through training, too. But then Roy got the fever that made him spend his war in the Navy Hospital.

Our train ride to Seattle would be a "big adventure," my mom said.

I can only remember two things that happened, other than an endless parade of bologna sandwiches—with no mustard, because Mom said I'd drip it on my clothes and, besides, "It is not good for you." Grandpa Homer—Dad's father, who lived in Montana—ate it on his sandwiches, and he said, "It don't hurt me none." I loved how Grandpa Homer looked at things.

Anyway, the two non-bologna things that I remember happening on the way to Seattle were that our train ran head-on into another train, and a man introduced himself as Mr. Smith and became a pest to Mom.

The man walked through our car, looking everyone up and down. He wore a dark blue suit, with a white shirt and a red and yellow tie. Mom was looking out the window as she usually did, and didn't notice him. I noticed him. I noticed everything. But I said nothing.

The man seemed to be up to something. He came back through and sat a few seats away, but I noticed he was watching me and Mom.

I got hungry and asked Mom for a sandwich. She dug out a bologna sandwich from the bag of them that she'd made for us to eat on this trip. There'd also been two apples and an orange and a Hershey Bar, but they were long gone. I got up to get a tiny cup of stale water to drink from the end of the car to wash down the sandwich, and when I got back, the man was in my seat, talking to Mom.

I stood there with my little cup of water.

Finally, the man noticed me. "Oh, is this your seat, Young Man?"

At least he didn't call me "Little Man." I hated that. "Yes," I said.

"Yes, what?" Mom asked.

"Yes, it's my seat."

"Yes, Sir," Mom said.

I said nothing.

"He's going through a difficult stage," Mom said. "You'll have to excuse him"

"Oh, I do. I've gone through some difficult stages myself. Here's your seat back, Young Man." He moved to a seat across from and facing us.

I sat down and began eating my sandwich with one hand. I held the little paper cup of water in the other hand.

"That sandwich looks swell," the man said.

I kept chewing and said nothing.

Mom said, "We've got a bag full of them. Would you like one?"

"I've got a better idea," the man said. "Why don't the three of us go back to the dining car and eat that fried chicken dinner they're offering today? My treat. Just for the pleasure of your company. I miss my little boy back home in Duluth. I'd love your company."

I thought he'd never stop talking.

"Oh, we couldn't do that," Mom said. "It wouldn't be right."

"You'd be doing me a favor. I'm a lonely man on a mission for the government, and it's just a meal."

"Really?" Mom said. "A mission for the government? A secret mission?"

"I can't really talk about it."

I thought to myself, *Then he shouldn't have brought it up.* But I knew better than to say that out loud. I'd been slapped for less. Not by my mom, but by another strange man in San Diego. So I kept my mouth shut.

"Oh," my mom said. "That makes sense."

It made no sense to me, but I held off on eating the bologna sandwich, just in case Mom decided to take up his offer of the chicken dinner.

"Well, I guess it wouldn't hurt anything to go to the dining car and eat fried chicken," she said. "That seems harmless enough." I suspected she was as tired of bologna sandwiches as I was. Maybe more tired. I knew we had almost no money, as our train fare had gobbled up most of what Mom had.

"Beyond harmless," the man said. Whatever that meant.

So we got up and followed the man to the dining room car. It was a few cars away, and we went through a lot of those heavy doors and got some chilly fresh air, as we were briefly in the open and were high in the mountains.

There was an empty table with a little sign on it. The man ushered Mom and me to sit down at the table. "Oh, but this table is 'reserved,'" Mom said.

"It's okay. It's reserved for me," the man said.

Soon the dining car steward was there, seating us formally. He called the man Mr. Smith. I saw Mr. Smith pass the Negro man what looked like money.

"Yes, Suh, thank you, Suh," the black man said.

"We'd like three of those chicken dinners, Edward," Mr. Smith said.

"Yes, Suh. Right away, Suh."

We sat and looked out the window at the mountain scenery. Mr. Smith turned to Mom. "So, where are you headed?"

"Seattle," Mom said.

"Joining your husband up there, are you?"

"No, he's in the Marines."

"I suppose he's somewhere in the Pacific Theater killing Japs," he said.

"Yes, he is."

About this time, our chicken dinners arrived. Each of us also got a little plate that had a big biscuit on it. There was a dish of pieces of butter and a little jar of honey with a spoon in it. The big plates we each got had a fried chicken drumstick and slices of white meat, and mashed potatoes and gravy and a mound of bright green peas. I had not seen a plate of food like this since we'd last had dinner at Grandma's in Ballard. I didn't know what to eat first, so I sat there and watched Mom and Mr. Smith.

"Well, let's dig in, shall we?" said Mr. Smith.

Mom said, "Yes."

I said nothing. I just picked up the chicken drumstick and started eating the crispy skin. It was really good. I hoped I would never have to eat another bologna sandwich, mustard or no mustard. The mashed potatoes and gravy were good, too. That big biscuit was the best, and the honey and the butter didn't hurt it at all.

"Eat your peas," Mom said. "They're better with butter and salt and pepper."

She was right, but I liked the chicken and mashed potatoes and gravy best. We all cleaned our plates. We had apple pie for dessert, with a slice of cheddar cheese on it.

"You eat well for a little boy," Mr. Smith said.

I said nothing.

"What do you say?" Mom asked.

"Yes."

"Yes, Sir," Mom said.

"Yes, Sir."

Mr. Smith laughed. I didn't know what was funny.

After the meal, I felt tired. I told Mom. "It's time for his nap," she said.

"Good idea. I could use one, too," Mr. Smith said.

Mom and I made our way back to our car. We took our old seats. Well, not exactly. I stretched out on the seat across from where I'd been sitting with Mom. She put her coat over me. I fell asleep.

I didn't wake up until our train ran head-on into another train. The wreck threw me off the seat I was sleeping on and into my Mom's lap.

Mr. Smith was nowhere to be seen. There was big confusion and noise. One of the porters got hit on the head with a suitcase that fell off the overhead storage rack, and he died.

Eventually, we were put on another train that was sent out to rescue us. I never saw Mr. Smith again, and Mom never brought him up. I hoped he got to complete his secret government mission. It was a long time before I got another fried chicken dinner with apple pie for dessert. Cheese or no cheese.

It was good to get back to Ballard, to Grandma's boarding house and our room in the basement. I had my own little bed. I also had my little tin cars to play with in the dirt right by the kitchen door, where I could smell the cinnamon rolls that my grandma baked. I sat there in the dirt for hours, rain and shine, as Mom said.

Mostly rain. It was Seattle.

PILLAR, THREE: BALLARD REDUX

BACK HOME IN BALLARD

It was good to be home in Seattle. The warm drizzle fell nonstop on Grandma's small back yard, where I sat in the dirt, playing with my little tin cars and trucks. I had small pieces of scrap wood from the lumberyard my Grandpa used to work in before his heart attack. Now he stayed home and Grandma took in boarders to make ends meet. I used the pieces of wood to make garages and bridges and jump-offs for my cars and trucks.

Due to the war, Seattle was full of people looking for a place to stay. Men had streamed into Seattle from all over the west to get work at Boeing. My father had been one of those. He'd left the Montana School of Mines in Butte behind and come to Seattle to seek his fortune.

Now he was gone to be a Marine in the Pacific. His job was to kill Japs and keep them out of Seattle. The ones that had lived here were long gone, taken away to prisons for their crimes. And they weren't expected to ever return. Why would they want to return where they weren't wanted? My Aunt Lee said they would be tarred and feathered and rode out of town on rails if they dared to show their faces in Ballard.

Like Aunt Lee said, "If they wanted to live in peace in Seattle, they shouldn't have bombed Pearl Harbor." She also said, "Such sneaking and back-stabbing causes all bets to be off. They deserve whatever happens to them now."

One day, Mom showed me the house a few blocks from Grandma's where a Japanese family had lived until soldiers came with guns and trucks to load them up and take them away. The house was just like the one my parents had lived in in Ballard, the house they were in when I was born. But now it was a wreck. All the windows were broken out and boarded up. The real Americans in Ballard were outraged that a Japanese family lived amongst them.

Most of the real Americans were of very recent Norwegian and Swedish origin, and spoke English with what my mother called "a brogue." My mother's family was one of those real American families.

My grandfather left Norway when he was in his twenties, went to Canada, and then came to America. He told stories of dancing on the wharfs that projected into the fjords, and falling drunk into the icy water.

Grandmother was death on alcohol consumption. She was the eldest child of her family, and had been saddled with raising her four brothers, as her parents were busy with the farm in Poulsbo, across the sound from Seattle. All but one of those brothers chose salmon and halibut fishing as their way of earning a living. The exception was her brother John—Uncle Johnny. He hated fishing, and went to Waterville and bought a few thousand acres of land to raise wheat on.

All of the brothers, according to Grandma Alma, were drunks. Perhaps they were, or perhaps they just drank some beer on festive occasions. I'll never know.

I do know that on Christmas in Seattle, they'd show up late for the gift exchange ritual, smelling of alcohol and with bright red faces. And Grandma, their big sister, would throw a fit. Grandma never minded making a scene, even on Christmas Eve. In fact, she seemed to love having an excuse to make a big fuss.

All her brothers resented their sister Alma, and told tales of how she abused them when they were small boys. My mother told those tales, too. Mom showed me scars on her ankles where Grandma had beaten her with a stick of kindling until the blood ran down into her socks.

Grandma had always been kind to me. The person she seemed meanest to was Grandpa Hulver. After him came Mom. Grandma seemed to live for being able to get after them both at the same time. That opportunity came when she smelled wine on Grandpa's breath after he'd come down to visit me and Mom in our basement room.

Mom said that "Daddy came down to tipple."

He kept a bottle of sweet wine in the back of our closet. I'd found it in there one day when I was digging around, looking for something to play with. Mom wasn't happy with my discovery. "Put that back and leave it alone and pretend you never found it. That's none of your business. You are always into everything."

I heard that a lot. When we visited relatives, I liked to rummage in the bottom cupboards I could reach and get out the pots and pans. This had always annoyed Aunt Lee especially. She had no kids. She went on record to say, "When I have kids, they'll respect other peoples' property and not get into things."

I wonder if she ever thought of this later, when she and Roy, who had by then recovered from the fever that kept him out of the war theater, adopted Michael, who had the same respect for property that Frank and Jesse James showed for banks and railroads. I doubt it. People lose their memories when they have kids like Michael. Also, they lose their patience and their minds.

Where was I? Grandpa had bad habits. He was Norwegian, born and raised there. He used snus, a Swedish tobacco snuff; he slurped hot coffee through a sugar cube out of a saucer, and he liked to drink sweet wine. He stashed the sweet wine in our closet because it was not safe upstairs where Grandma ruled the domain. He couldn't get to the wine in our closet easily; nothing in the house moved without a blessing from Grandma.

I don't know how Grandpa even managed to buy the wine and smuggle it into the house and hide it in our closet. When I asked my mother about that, decades later, she had no clue and no interest. She did recollect Grandma's Alma's wrath, though, and the incident that ultimately led to our taking the train to Thompson Falls to stay with Dad's parents.

Grandpa had been visiting us and he'd poured a glass of the wine. He drank it from an old jelly glass. The wine was very purple and smelled like grape juice gone bad. Grandpa and I sat on our sofa in front of an old trunk we used as a coffee table. Grandpa had brought his world globe with him, because he knew one of my favorite things to do was to have him point out the countries he'd been to and tell me stories about them.

To refresh my memory concerning the globe, I've fetched it from my study, where it sits on a bookshelf. I've placed it on the kitchen table under the harsh kitchen light, where I can see that it is pretty beat up. There's a white spot to the east of Greenland where the blue ocean has peeled off. Long ago, someone drew a circle around Norway, my grandpa's homeland.

The globe has a legend on it that reads, "12 inch standard Globe made by Replogle Globes, Chicago, Ill. Clear, accurate, up to date." I could find no date on it, but it had to be from the late 1930's. The amazing thing is that this old globe exists at all. When Grandpa died, I was still a little kid, and when I was asked if there was a memento of Grandpa that I wanted, I asked for the globe. I've hung onto it ever since.

It's all I've got of Grandpa that he and I enjoyed together.

How many times have I moved since he died? I've lost count. But I remember that day, and other days, when we sat together on the sofa and he showed me Norway and Sweden and Greenland and told me Viking tales. How they built little wooden boats and journeyed to Scotland and even farther. He showed me Africa, and said they made it there, too.

My mind was filled with the possibilities of the world by Grandpa Hulver and his tales of travel. He pointed out the Islas Canaries and Cabo Verde and said Vikings went there, too. "You can do anything you put your mind to," he told me. My life didn't seem that way then, but I thought, Maybe later.

Grandpa finished his jelly glass of sweet wine, rinsed his glass out in our sink, and patted me on the head. "If I don't get back upstairs soon, she'll come and hunt me down. We don't want that."

We all knew who "she" was. No, we didn't want her storming down here. Mom was upstairs with her at the time, helping her cook dinner for the boarders. Grandpa had said, sniffing the air, "It smells like corned beef and cabbage." It was a dish we both liked, but it smelled better in the kitchen. Down here in the basement, it didn't smell like dinner, but something worse. Maybe only the bad smells sank this low, and the good buttery and peppery smells stayed in the kitchen. Another mystery.

Grandpa left the globe on the coffee table, so I sat there, playing a game I'd devised. I'd shut my eyes, twirl the globe, and when it stopped, I'd stab it with a finger, open my eyes and see where I'd ended up. At four, I couldn't read, but I'd memorized many of the places on the globe while being shown stuff by Grandpa.

This time, my finger stabbed in an area above a bunch of islands, above a large area that Grandpa had told me was Australia. "That's where the kangaroos live," Grandpa had told me. That had stuck in my mind. Grandpa got a yellow magazine in the mail called National

Geographic, and he had dug out one of them that had an article in it on Australia that showed pictures of kangaroos. I decided then that, when I grew up, I would go to Australia.

A few minutes after Grandpa went upstairs, I heard a lot of hollering. First my Grandma. Then Grandpa. Then Mom. Then I heard feet pounding down the stairs. I didn't want to be a part of this. I ducked down behind the sofa before they got to our basement room.

"Where have you got that wine bottle hid, Hulver?" I heard my Grandmother shout. She smacked Hulver a couple of times with her open hand. Hulver said nothing.

"Alice, you know where it is. Where is it hid?" Grandma smacked Mom a couple of times, too.

Neither Grandpa nor Mom seemed inclined to tell.

Grandma opened the closet door, bent over and rooted around behind the stuff on the floor, mostly shoes. "There it is. You can't fool me. You are both stupids," she said. She took the bottle, went to the sink, removed the cork, and poured what little wine was left in the bottle down the drain. "Don't you two ever try to fool me again. It won't work. I'm too smart for you. Alice, I'll talk to you later. Hulver, you come with me."

Grandma Alma was a large, loud woman, and very scary when she made an effort to be. She grabbed Grandpa by the scruff of his neck and dragged him out of our room and up the stairs. I heard the sounds of her hitting him when she got him upstairs.

I crept out from behind the sofa.

Mom and I looked at each other.

"This isn't working out," Mom said.

THE COCONUT

I sat in the dirt, just outside the kitchen door of my grandmother's boarding house. I was playing with my little cars and trucks, building ramps and tunnels with scrap bits of kindling that my Grandfather Hulver had brought home from the lumberyard where he used to work, before his heart attacks.

I could hear the voices of my mother and grandmother rising and falling in the kitchen, where they were preparing lunch for the boarders. I could tell by the voices that they were angry at each other. Suddenly the voices stopped. A few minutes later, my mother came out of the door. Her face was red with anger.

"Put down your cars, Davy. We're leaving here right now," she said.

This was not a new situation for me. This happened again and again when we stayed at my grandma's in her basement. My mother and her mother had been at each other's throats forever. Grandma would tell my mother how it had to be, and my mother would refuse to do it that way. It was a contest of wills that neither would ever win. I just tried to avoid being caught in the middle.

"Yes, Mama. Where are we going?"

"Golden Gardens. To the beach," she said. She had her beach bag over one shoulder. It contained our beach stuff: a towel, swim trunks for me, a small bucket and a little shovel, and a book for Mom to read.

We walked down the concrete back stairs to the sidewalk. "Are we going to walk the whole way?" I asked.

"No, we'll take the bus the second half of the way."

"Good."

I was almost four, but I wasn't much of a walker. It made my feet hurt. I didn't want to be carried, but walking was hard for me. A year or so later, I quit walking, and when my feet were x-rayed, it was discovered that my feet were defective—missing crucial bones. My father fainted dead away when the doctor delivered that news.

We walked up the block, past Ballard High School, where my mother had graduated not that long ago.

Every time we walked past Ballard High, she'd tell me the same story, almost as though she were talking to herself. "They made me take two years of French. I wanted to take Norwegian, but they wouldn't offer Norwegian. They said Norwegian had no serious literature, that Norwegian was not the language of the educated classes, but of fishermen and lumbermen."

Mom always got mad when she told that story. Today she was already angry at her mother. Mom's mouth went up in a tight little circle like it always did when I did something to displease her, such as being noisy in a public place or spilling milk at the table. "Be a good little boy. Nobody likes a noisy or messy little boy," she'd say.

No, nobody did. They scarcely put up with a quiet, neat little boy. Little boys were not in great demand during World War II. They were around only under sufferance.

"That French teacher hated me. And I hated her. She said my pronunciation of French sounded like I had my mouth full of lutefisk. She'd say 'Spit out the lutefisk and try that again, Alice.' She was so mean."

When we got to the shopping district of Ballard, we waited at the stop for the bus that would take us to Golden Gardens. It was only another mile or two, but my feet were done by then.

I enjoyed the bus ride. I liked looking out the window at the boats at the Marina. We got out at Golden Gardens. The light drizzle had stopped and the sun came out. There was even some blue sky with big fluffy clouds. One of the clouds looked like a big barking dog. We found a place on the beach by a big log. Mom spread out the beach towel and sat down on it and began to read her library book. I played in the sand with my shovel and little bucket. I built a sand tower.

I heard the train whistle in the distance. "Can we go stand under the overpass in the tunnel when the train comes?"

"Sure," Mom said. She put her library book down on the towel. We walked over to the tunnel under the train tracks, and I stood there holding my mother's hand and waited for the train to thunder overhead.

Soon it did. We weren't the only ones there by then. There were two other moms with their little girls in tow. Everyone—well, the kids—screamed as the train passed right overhead, rattling the tracks and the tunnel and shaking dust and little bits of gravel onto our heads. What a thrill it was.

And then the train was gone. Silence reigned.

We walked back to our beach towel. We stopped on the way at the snackbar, and Mom got me a hot dog. I got extra mustard and relish. The hot dog was on a nice soft bun. I sat on the log and watched the water for whales as I ate my hot dog. I saw lots of boats, but no whales.

After I finished the hot dog, Mom wiped the mustard off my mouth. "That's why you shouldn't get mustard." She wiped hard on my chin with a spit-dampened hanky.

"But I love mustard."

"It makes a mess," she said.

Yes, it did, but it was the main reason I liked hotdogs at the beach. The mustard. Also the relish and the soft bun. At home when we got hotdogs, we got them with bread and no mustard or relish. "Hotdog buns cost too much. Money is tight. They are just bread," Mom would say.

Hotdogs need buns, mustard and relish. I told myself that, when I grew up, I'd always eat them that way.

The drizzle started again, so Mom shook the sand out of our stuff and put it away in her beach bag. She took my hand and we walked over to the bus stop.

We rode the bus to where we'd gotten on and walked the rest of the way to Grandma's house.

We went in the basement door to avoid the kitchen. Grandpa was waiting for us. He was sitting on the old sofa that was our main piece of furniture. In front of him on the coffee table was an odd-shaped brown object, sort of like a football.

"You got mail from your daddy, Davy," Grandpa said.

"What is it?"

"What does it look like?"

"I don't know," I said. "Sort of like a big nut."

"You're right, Davy. It's a coconut," Grandpa said.

"A coconut?"

"Yes, a coconut. Sit down by me, and let's look at it."

There was a white cardboard label attached to a wire that went through a hole in the end of the coconut. "There's your name on the mailing label—'Davy Willson'—and this address," Grandpa said. He showed me the label, but I couldn't make heads or tales out of it.

But I was thrilled to have received mail from my daddy. It's the only piece of mail I have left from the many letters he sent me during World War II. The mailing label is long gone, but the coconut sits in front of me as I write these words.

"Look at what's painted on the coconut," Grandpa said. There were yellow words on its brown, shiny skin. There was a yellow palm tree on a small yellow island. Two seabirds in the sky and a circle of sun, with rays poking out from it.

"What do the words say, Grandpa?"

"'Guam 45,'" Grandpa said.

"That's where Daddy is."

"Yes, that's where he was when he mailed the coconut, and the '45' is the year 1945. You were born in 1942."

"Will my daddy be home soon?"

"We hope he will," Grandpa said.

"Where is Guam?"

Grandpa's globe was sitting on our coffee table. He whirled the globe and pointed to a tiny dot surrounded by blue ocean. "Right there, Davy. It's one of the islands in the Marianas, that string of dots that are islands. See that word there? 'J—A—P'? It spells 'Jap.'"

"Yes, Dad's out there to kill them," I said.

"Yes, he is. The Japs owned all those islands. And they dug in on them, and they had to be rooted out. But mostly they are out now. That's why your dad sent you that coconut. The fighting is over. You should hang on to this big nut. It's a keepsake," Grandpa said. "Like a souvenir."

"Okay," I said. "I'll try."

I've hung onto that coconut now for many decades. That coconut, and the old beat-up world globe that Grandpa Hulver and I spent so many hours studying together. Most of the world I knew then is long gone.

* * *

"It's time to come up for dinner," my grandmother hollered down the stairs at us.

We all looked at each other.

"Time to face the music," Grandpa said.

"And dance," Mom said.

"No dancing," Grandpa said.

"What's for dinner?" I asked.

"Macaroni and cheese," Grandpa said.

"Oh, I like that." I did. Grandma made it in a giant pan that looked too heavy to lift. But she could lift it easily. She had big, powerful arms.

Grandpa headed up the stairs. He was the slowest of us.

"Let's wash our hands, Davy," Mom said. We went over to our sink and washed our hands and, for good measure, my face. Mom also ran a comb through my hair. "You need a haircut, Davy."

"Okay," I said.

We walked up to dinner. The good smell of the macaroni and cheese led us up the stairs.

GRANDMA'S MACARONI AND CHEESE

When Mom and I got to the top of the stairs and entered the kitchen, Grandma Alma was rattling Norwegian at Grandpa Hulver, never a good sign. Mom and I sat down in our chairs at the kitchen table. Mine had a pillow lift on it that Grandpa had built for me so that I could reach the table easily to eat my food.

Everyone else was already at the table. Well, Grandma was standing by the stove. At the table were: Grandpa, Uncle Ludwig, three boarders—Bill, Jack, and Otto—and, of course, Mom and me. The table was all set and loaded with dishes of steaming hot food.

There was a huge pan, in the center, of macaroni and cheese, golden brown on top and dark in the corners; a big bowl of string beans with bacon, a bowl of fruit salad, and a bowl of boiled potatoes because Grandpa had to have potatoes at every meal. There was also a slab of butter on a dish, and salt and pepper. And a pot of hot coffee on the stove that Grandma Alma poured from.

Even though I'd had a hotdog at Golden Gardens that afternoon, I was very hungry. I loved Grandma's macaroni and cheese, especially the crisp and crackly cheesy edges where the cheese and the noodles were fused together.

Grandma sat down and said a short prayer in Norwegian, and dinner began. Everything was done in an orderly fashion as Grandma insisted, with no flurry and no rush or elbowing. My plate was dished up by my mother—mostly macaroni and cheese, with a few green beans and a small scoop of fruit salad. No potatoes. Some butter on my green beans.

The boarders were friends of Uncle Ludwig's, men he worked with at Boeing. One time, I'd asked Otto what he did at Boeing. He'd answered, "I could tell you, but then I'd have to kill you."

Mother has told me I fled from the table, and that she had a heck of a time getting me to eat breakfast the next morning. I was a very literal-minded little boy, and took his joke as a threat to my life. I never sat near or talked to Otto again.

I wondered what he did at Boeing that was so secret he'd threaten the life of a little boy? When Otto wasn't around, I asked Uncle Lud. He'd laughed, and said he was a "machine wiper." I asked what that meant, and Lud said, "He wipes down the oil and grease on the drill presses and the like with old rags."

"He wipes machines?"

"Yes, that's what he does."

I wondered for years what Otto really did.

Otto was a big eater. He loved Grandma's food, as did Bill and Jack. Uncle Ludwig had lured them all to Grandma's boarding house, as he had lured my father some years earlier, with the promise of good food and lots of it. Grandma did not disappoint.

Now he and Bill and Jack were eating Grandma's macaroni and cheese. Bill and Jack were also arguing about something. They did that a lot. They'd been told not to, but they couldn't help themselves. Bill had a big red face and what Grandma called "an Irish last name." Jack was a dark, skinny guy with a bad leg. His nickname behind his back was "Nig." When I'd asked him why he limped, he'd said, "I got this in the Great War, killing Huns." Later Uncle Lud told me he'd crippled his leg falling off a streetcar when he got drunk. I tended to believe Uncle Lud.

"The Japs are going to fight to the very last man for their Emperor and their Homeland," Jack said.

"Naw, they'll quit when they see that the Germans are whipped," Bill said. "They won't want Japan destroyed."

"Our Marines will have to go house to house in Tokyo and every other Jap city and town and kill them one by one with bayonets and flamethrowers," Jack said.

"That's enough of that talk," Grandma announced from the head of the table. "That's not fit dinner table conversation. I've warned you two in the past."

"So we gotta sit and eat your food without expressing opinions on current events?" Bill asked.

"Talk about the weather or a movie you've seen, not about the war. Davy's dad is a Marine. He doesn't need to hear that sort of talk. Neither do I," Grandma said.

"Well, fine," Bill said. "What's for dessert? There's no point in talking about the weather. It's raining, as per usual."

"Yeah, and we've been too busy working to see a movie," Jack said.

"Dessert is apple pie with a slice of cheddar cheese if you wish it," Grandma said.

One by one everyone but Mother spoke up for pie. Mother had said not one word at dinner, other than "Please" or "Thank you." I hadn't heard that much from Uncle Lud or Grandpa, either. They knew better than to open their mouths except to shovel food in or to drink coffee to wash the food down. I drank my milk and tried hard not to spill it.

Grandma Alma spoke to my mother. "So, Alice, what do you have to say for yourself?"

"I'll have apple pie, please, and I'll help serve it to the others. Also, tomorrow, Davy and I are taking the train to Thompson Falls."

All was quiet around the large kitchen table. Everyone looked at Mother and me. No reason to look at me; it was a surprise to me, too, although I'd expected something to happen after Grandma threw that fit about Grandpa keeping a bottle of wine hidden in our basement apartment that he would "tipple" on, to use Mother's word. Mother did not like being told what to do. Right after that happened, she'd said, more to herself than to me, "I'd rather live in a boxcar in that one-horse town (She'd meant Thompson Falls, Montana) than stay here in Seattle and be treated like I'm still a small child."

Grandma treated everyone like they were small children, not just Mom, but Mom and Grandma had never gotten along. Mom was the baby of her family, and I'd heard it said that Grandma thought that two children were more than enough. Lud and Aleda were the first two, so it was obvious where that left Mom.

Both Uncle Lud and Aunt Lee told me that. Even Grandpa Hulver told me that. "When your Grandma gets her tail in a knot, there's no dealing with her. And your mother never would say 'Uncle.' She'd die first, and a couple of times I was afraid it would come to that."

Mom served us all warm apple pie, with warmed cheddar cheese on top for those who wanted it. Most did. I even did, and I usually didn't like anything parked on top of my food. We all dug in. Bill and Jack were done in no time and asked for seconds, which they got. Grandma had made three apple pies. And she had a giant block of cheddar cheese on the sideboard.

Otto had only one piece of pie, but he'd loaded up on macaroni and cheese. He liked it as much as I did. And he liked the crispy parts, too. But Mom had made sure to dish those up on my plate so I'd not miss out.

* * *

Tomorrow we'd travel by train to Montana, and we'd soon be back in Thompson Falls. I liked it there. I liked living in a boxcar right by the tracks and the train depot. My cousin Laila lived nearby, and we'd play in the sandbox Grandpa Homer had built me from railroad ties. It didn't rain as much in Thompson Falls, so we could play in the sandbox most any time we wanted to.

I liked riding the train. I also looked forward to the war ending, and my dad coming home, and our living together in one spot. All the moving around was confusing, and I always felt I was in the way. My grandpas were always good to me and spent time with me, but everyone else seemed busy with what they called the "war effort."

The "war effort" was very serious. When I asked Uncle Lud about it, he'd looked at me and said, "Loose lips sink ships."

I thought about that a long time. What could that mean? It sounded like a short poem. But it made no more sense to me than "The little dog laughed to see such a sport, and the dish ran away with the spoon." What? Adults were always saying stuff like that to me. And they didn't like answering questions about it, either. So I learned to not do that. But where was the sense in it? Loose lips sink ships?

I knew I wouldn't ask Otto about that one. Or Jack or Bill, either. None of them had time for a little boy. Mom had even told me to steer clear of Bill. When I'd asked why, she'd just said, "Just steer of him. Especially when he's in his cups."

So I did as she said, although I never knew when he was in his cups or out of them. I heard Grandma say once of Bill, "Those Irish have a problem. He smells like a hot mince pie. But I need his money."

The next day, Mom and I took the city bus to the train depot downtown, dragging along our little striped suitcase. The depot was crowded with men in uniform. And some women, too. We got on the train and settled into a seat. Mom let me sit next to the window. There was nothing much in the world I liked better than looking out of a train window. I loved seeing the back yards of towns and cities — the warehouses and stockyards crowded with animals.

I occupied myself with the view until I dozed off.

I woke up hours later, and it was dark when I looked out the window. I saw only the stars. "When will we get to Thompson Falls, Mom?"

"Next time you wake up, we'll be there."

And she was right.

Grandpa Homer was there waiting for us. He carried me home to the boxcar and tucked me into my little bed. It was good to be there. I loved the wood-smoke smell of the place, and I looked forward to getting up in the morning and going out to the kitchen to help Grandpa drink his coffee, smoke his cigarette and read his newspaper. He'd read Alley Oop to me and fry me an egg if I wanted one. And he'd make me a piece of toast, too, with lots of butter and huckleberry jam. That was the last thing in my mind that night, as I drifted off to sleep.

POST, FOUR: THOMPSON FALLS

BOXCARS IN THOMPSON FALLS, MONTANA

And so, we took the train from Seattle to Thompson Falls, Montana.

There, we lived with Dad's parents, Grandpa and Grandma Willson, next to the tracks in boxcars. When the trains rolled by, everything in our little home shook. I had a sandbox to play in with my little cars, and my distant cousin Laila, who lived nearby with her mother. Her father was gone to the war, too, and my grandparents and my mom took care of her sometimes.

Laila and I played in the sandbox together for hours. That was fun, and is a great memory, aided now by a black-and-white photo of the two of us in that sandbox made of railroad ties. Laila was like a sister to me during that time; she grew up to be a lovely young woman, but she stayed in Montana, and I did not live there for long after the war.

Mom was glad to get away from her mother. She said she hated to be "under Mom's thumb."

One day Mom was out in the field near the tracks with a broom, swatting grasshoppers to be used for bait for trout when we went fishing with Grandpa. I was there, too, helping her put the bugs into Prince Albert tobacco cans. A troop train rolled into the station and stopped. The hundreds of soldiers on the train flocked to the windows to hoot and holler at my mom, out in the field in cut-off jeans and a shirt tied up at the waist.

The soldiers started chanting, "Daisy Mae, Daisy Mae," at Mom.

"What are they saying?" Mom asked me.

"'Daisy Mae,'" I said.

"What does that mean?"

"From Li'l Abner."

"What's that?"

Mom was not a fan of newspaper comic strips. I was a big fan, thanks to my grandpa Homer, who loved them. He read them every day. I'd sit on his lap as he smoked his first morning Camel, drank his cup of coffee, and read the comics. Li'l Abner was our favorite. I always hoped that when I grew up, I could visit Lower Slobovia. I think I suspected it was a made-up place, existing only in the artist's mind. But maybe not.

Suddenly, in Thompson Falls on a summer morning, I was transported to Lower Slobovia, or at least to Dogpatch, where Li'l Abner and Daisy Mae lived.

As a four-year-old, I was often in the position of trying to explain things I hardly understood to my mom, who didn't understand them at all. She was never quick on the uptake at anything new to her. So I explained to her that the soldiers thought she was Daisy Mae from Dogpatch come alive in Thompson Falls.

Mom was not happy at this. "I'm a Seattle girl. I'm not some country girl," she said. "I guess we have enough grasshoppers." And we left the field next to the tracks, and carried our broom and our Prince Albert cans back to our boxcar home.

The Prince Albert can I carried home was full of grasshoppers. I could hear them scratching in there. There were holes punched in the can so they could breathe.

* * *

Later in the day, we went fishing with Grandpa at a nearby stream. We didn't catch any fish. I didn't care, as I didn't fish anyhow. I liked to spend my time by the cool stream, avoiding rattlesnakes and looking for dry flies that fishermen had left behind when they got snarled in the brush. I had a Prince Albert can that I kept my dry fly collection in. I had quite a few stored in there, along with a few inches of the line they were tied to.

On the way back from the stream, we stopped at the drug store, which had a big soda fountain and many flavors of ice cream. I got chocolate, as I usually did. I walked down the sidewalk to the phone company office, where my grandmother was on duty that day as a telephone operator. My grandpa and Mom stayed behind in the drugstore. I popped in and said hello to Grandma, who sat at the switchboard with her head in the earphones she wore. I let her have a lick of my cone, and walked back down the sidewalk to the drugstore.

We loaded up in the Chevy and drove the short blocks to the boxcars we lived in. We could have easily walked, but we had the car, as we'd needed it to get to the stream where we had fished.

That afternoon I spent with my grandpa out in the yard. He and I were working on my learning all the songs that he knew, and we had a long way to go. So far I'd learned *De Camp Town Races*, *Old Dan Tucker*, *I've Been Working on the Railroad*, *I Don't Want No More of Army Life*, *Hobo Bill*, *The Railroad Man*, *The Yellow Rose of Texas*, *Oh Susannah*, *She'll Be Coming 'Round the Mountain*, *Hallelujah I'm a Bum*, *John Jacob Jingleheimer Schmidt*, and *The Sinking of the Titanic*. Grandpa knew hundreds of songs. He'd learned a lot of them from his brothers, and some from his father, Homer Senior.

Grandpa had a lot of railroad ties, like the ones he had used to build me the sandbox, stacked near the boxcar, and for years the smell of creosote reminded me of that box and of the songs Grandpa taught me. I guess it still does. It never occurred to me that creosote might be an unfriendly chemical that caused problems for some folks. It was just a constant part of the world of people who lived right by the tracks of the NPRR.

It seemed a good life to me. I loved the trains rumbling past on a strict schedule, although Grandpa said that the war had disrupted that schedule and now you never knew for sure when a train full of troops headed for Europe or Asia might show up at the station. A couple of times, he'd been caught out on the tracks in that little car he rode in to do his duties as a signal maintainer and track inspector. He had to bail off the car fast and pull it free, or get "pulverized," he said. I loved that word. Grandpa had a lot of words like that.

His mother had been a schoolteacher, and she taught Homer and his brothers at home in their sod house in Brocksburg, Nebraska, in Keya Paha County, where he'd been born. Brocksburg was a town that was no longer there. Grandpa said he once went back, and all that was there was wind blowing through, and a little cemetery that had a few white graves in it of babies that hadn't made it out of Nebraska.

He and his family had come to Montana from Nebraska in a wagon, and had settled on a little farm not far from Missoula, in Lolo, a tiny little place that Grandpa called a "wide spot in the road; not even a one-horse town." He'd say, "Dogs would sleep in the middle of the main street." I loved to listen to my Grandpa talk, tell stories and sing.

I always wondered why my father never talked or told stories or sang.

"That's not who he is," my mom would say. "He's a man of few words."

"Yes, and those are not pleasant," Aunt Nellie Mae would add. "They are warnings or admonitions." Nellie Mae was my only aunt on this side of the family, Father's baby sister.

"Did he look out for you the way my big brother Lud did for me?'"
Mother asked her.

"Look out for me? He had me crushed under his thumb. He
would not let me have any fun at all. I couldn't go to a party, or
go swimming in the river," Nellie Mae said. "Pop was that way too.
'You'll get polio if you swim in that dirty river,' he'd say. And of
course, he was right. Some kids did get polio. Pop was worried sick
about everything, but especially about us getting polio. He never
gave that a rest."

Nellie Mae was more fun than Mom's sister, Aunt Lee. Aunt Lee
was okay, but she was as dark and gloomy as my dad. Worse, lots of
days.

Still, Nellie Mae did have that side to her, too. I heard her say one
day that she thought that we weren't destined for hell, that we were
there already, that life on earth was hell. She also thought that the
war would never end, that the Japs might win. And if they lost, we'd
have to kill every last one of them before they would "throw in the
towel." I pictured that in my mind. All those Japs throwing towels.

I heard Nellie Mae say that one day my father would be fighting
house to house in Tokyo, if he survived Iwo.

Hearing that stuff filled me with gloom.

My mom always wanted to take my picture with a little Brownie
camera she had, and she always would say, "Smile!" I never did, and
that drove Mom nuts. Although what she said was, "You drive me to
distraction." But what was there to smile about? Not much. So my
photos from that period, and from later periods, too, seldom show
me smiling.

My favorite photo of me as a kid was taken when we were living in
Ballard, and they took me to Golden Gardens where the beach was,
and plopped me down on the beach, facing the salt water.

I'm wearing a corduroy jumper with a striped tee shirt under it.
I'm not dressed for the beach. My hair is down on my forehead and
my face is set between a frown and a bemused expression that was

common to it during that period and later. Looming in the background is a hill, Ballard Heights, I think, covered with fir trees. I am like a giant toddler in the photo. Back behind my left shoulder is Aunt Florence, and next to her is Uncle Ludwig. They are tiny, but more in focus than I am.

I am sure my mother crouched down in front of me, about a foot away, and took the picture, and she must have focused on the adults in the background, as I am fuzzy and Florence is clear. To Florence's right is a large bottle that looks as though it contains alcohol. I don't get that, as my family and Lud's were all teetotalers. Maybe that bottle just washed up on the sand. My mother wrote on the back of the photo, "Taken on the beach in Seattle, 1944." We were there for a going away party for my father, she told me.

The only beaches in Thompson Falls related to the Thompson River. Nothing like Golden Gardens. The only time we were on river beaches was when Mom and I went trout fishing with Grandpa.

One time I asked Grandma Katherine why she didn't come along with us.

"I'm too fat. Can you see me climbing over those rocks, sliding down those steep banks, to get to the creeks?"

"I guess not," I said. Although when it was mushroom season, she was pretty spry, and got more than her fair share of the mushrooms. I'd seen her jump over a barbwire fence to get to some burned-over area where she'd had good luck with mushrooms the season before. When we went huckleberry picking, she filled her bucket up faster than any of us.

I think Grandma just didn't like to fish, or to spend much time with Grandpa.

Mom and Grandpa loved fishing for trout, and both of them caught a lot of fish. Mother and Grandpa got along great, so they were fun to be with. They were easygoing together and not at all dark and gloomy.

I wished my dad were more like Grandpa, but that's not how things worked. I'd like to think my father was more light-hearted and easygoing before the Marine Corps grabbed him.

But maybe not. I can remember him coming home during Basic Training to where Mom and I lived in California, right near Camp Pendleton. He was swearing and ranting that if the drill instructor made him jump off the high tower one more time in full field gear into the deep pool, he would punch him right in the face. Mother was fearful that that would happen. What would happen to us if he spent the war in a Navy brig?

I don't remember Dad ever being mellow. He seemed always to be inches away from rage, and smashing stuff with a hammer if one was available, and he stayed that way as long as I knew him. Luckily, the Navy never made him jump off that tower again, so he didn't go to the brig.

No, Mother swears Dad was never much like Grandpa. But Nellie Mae says Grandpa was more like Dad when he was young.

So Dad and thousands of other Marines were shipped to Guam and then to Iwo Jima. How did we know where he was? He and his dad had a code. When Grandpa got a letter addressed to Homer G. Willson, we knew Dad was on Guam. Later, Grandpa got a letter addressed to Homer I. Willson, so we knew that Dad was on Iwo Jima. It wasn't so good to know that.

The daily newspapers printed Iwo stories and casualty reports. The early stories told us that, due to Navy artillery bombardment, few Japs would be alive on Iwo to fight when the Marines landed. Later, the news stories told us the Japs had spent months digging into the island. They wouldn't come out and fight. They killed Marines by the thousands when the men left the Navy ships in little boats to land on the beaches. The Marines couldn't get out of the water and over the edge of the beach onto the island to fight.

The mood in the boxcars then was dark. I heard Aunt Nellie Mae say to Mom that there was no way Bob could survive Iwo. And if he did, what shape would he be in to land in Japan and fight the millions of Japanese there?

I figured I'd never see my dad again. I sat for hours with Laila in the sandbox, building bunkers and pillboxes and tunnels for my trucks and cars to hide in. I made guns out of pieces of pipe and old metal that I found lying around by the railroad tracks. The field Mom and I hunted grasshoppers in had lots of nifty stuff in it, too.

One time, I found a dynamite cap and brought it home to show Grandpa. Grandpa took it from me and then demonstrated what it could do. I'm glad I didn't pound it with a rock. I would have lost the hand that held the rock.

I was always a lucky kid that way. If asked what kind of childhood I had, I would say it was a lucky one. Was it happy? I guess so. Why didn't I smile more for photos? Was I smiling on the inside? No, I wasn't. I was a sober kid. I was a kid surrounded by adults who were not a happy bunch.

My happiest times were with my grandpa Homer.

He had a shoebox full of postcards from his time in the Army, during WWI. We'd sit together and look through them. Some of the postcards showed ditches full of dead bodies. Grandpa called them "insurrectos." Some of the postcards were of Grandpa as a young man, in his Army uniform. In one of them, he had a .45 on his hip. He'd been in the Army in the Philippines in 1910. I asked him if he'd ever had to jump off a high tower into a deep pool wearing full gear, and he said no, "That's the Navy that does that stuff."

"How about the Marines?" I asked.

"They're just a part of the Navy."

I decided right then that if a war came my way, and if I had a choice, I'd follow Grandpa into the Army. He told me that two of his brothers and their father had all served in the Army.

* * *

Some 20 years later, a war did come my way. I was asked if I would become a Marine, and I said no — I would join the Army. And I did.

I'm told that when I was a baby, after I learned to say "Mama" and "Daddy," my next words were "Semper Fi."

I think that was just a bad joke.

BREAKFAST WITH GRANDPA HOMER

I had been sleeping in my bed in the boxcar the morning after we arrived in Thompson Falls. As I started to wake up, I smelled Grandpa Homer's morning rituals—his coffee, his cigarette—and I could hear him rustle the newspaper. I slipped out of bed and walked around the corner into the kitchen.

"Good morning, Captain," Grandpa called. That was a typical morning greeting from Grandpa Homer. It was the first line to a song he sometimes sang to me.

"Good morning, Grandpa," I said.

"You want some wake-up coffee, Podner?"

"Yes, please."

He poured some coffee into a cup, but not very much, and topped it off with milk from the bottle sitting on the kitchen table. "There you go. Climb up on your chair and drink up, Davy."

I climbed up and sipped the warm mixture.

"You want me to make you breakfast? You look hungry, Davy. You probably didn't get much to eat on that Number 2 train," Grandpa said.

"I'd like a hen in a hole, Grandpa," I said. "Please."

"You like that one? That's a special one. Since this is your first morning back in Thompson Falls in a while, I can whip that one up for you. I'd better put another log on the fire." He got a log out of the woodbin next to the front door, opened the door on the woodstove and shoved it in and poked it with the poker. Sparks flew up. When he got it where he wanted it, he closed the stove door.

He got an egg out of the icebox and took the black cast iron skillet down off its hook on the wall by the sink. He put it on top of the stove and put a big piece of butter in the pan. "Watch that butter and let me know when it begins to melt, Davy."

"Okay, Grandpa." I scooted my chair over near the stove and climbed up to stand on it so I had a good view of the butter in the pan.

"It's starting to melt, Grandpa," I said in a couple of minutes.

"Okay." He came and moved the skillet over to what he called the cool side of the stove. You still wouldn't want to put your hand on it. "Do you want to do the honors on the piece of bread?"

"I do," I said.

"Okie-dokie." He got out a piece of bread from the bag in the breadbox and put it on the wooden cutting board. He handed me a water glass. I scooted my chair over to the counter and once again climbed up so I could center the glass on the bread and cut a perfect circle out of the slice.

"Great!" Grandpa said.

He slid the cast iron skillet back onto the hot side of the stove, placed the bread with the hole in it into the hot butter, and handed me the egg. "Break the egg into the hole, Davy, the way I taught you."

I cracked the egg on the edge of the skillet and dumped it into the hole.

Grandpa plopped the leftover circle of bread into the pan next to the hen in the hole. He handed me the pepper shaker and I peppered the egg. Then the salt.

The egg and toast sizzled in the pan and the smell made my tummy growl. I had not had a real meal since I ate macaroni and cheese at Grandma Alma's in Ballard. Mostly, I had been eating bologna sandwiches with no mustard.

This was my favorite breakfast, maybe my favorite meal.

Grandpa got a spatula and flipped both pieces of bread over and then moved the frying pan to the other side of the stove. "Scoot your chair over to the table and I'll serve you your breakfast."

"Okay, Grandpa," I said.

He got a blue plate out of the cupboard and used the spatula to put my breakfast on it. Then he put the plate full of food in front of me. There was a jar of huckleberry jam already on the table with a spoon in it. I spooned jam onto my round piece of toast, and used the spoon to spread it around.

Grandpa sat down at the table with me, and picked up his coffee cup. "Breakfast is served, Captain. Dig in."

He handed me a fork and I dug in. Best breakfast ever. I didn't have to use the fork much, as it was like eating a sandwich. Grandpa didn't have all the rules for eating that Mom and Grandma had. He didn't have most rules like they did. When I was playing outside in the sandbox and had to go to the bathroom, he told me it was silly for me to go all the way inside when there was a big bush right handy.

When I finished eating, Grandpa and I washed up the dishes in the sink, and he dried them off with an old dishtowel and put them away in the cupboard. "Never leave evidence behind, Davy. Always keep 'em guessing," he said.

"Okay, Grandpa."

He poured another cup of coffee and made me a new cup of milk colored with some hot coffee. He gave me a couple of sugar cubes to put in mine and a spoon to stir with. Then he lit up another Camel to go with his coffee. He used a wooden kitchen match. "Promise me you'll never smoke, Davy," he said.

"Okay, Grandpa. Why not?"

"Tobacco is a dirty weed, Davy. Bad for your health."

"Why did you start smoking?"

"My older brothers all smoked, so I thought it was a good idea," he said. "It wasn't. Do you want to find out what Alley Oop's latest shenanigans are, Davy?"

"Yes, please."

Grandpa Homer had been reading me the Alley Oop comic strip as long as I could remember. I think Grandpa enjoyed Oop's adventures as much as I did. I loved the idea that a caveman could appear in modern times and do just fine. I also loved when he was back in caveman days, riding on Dinny the dinosaur.

Today Alley Oop was in yet another mess at the end of the strip, and we'd have to wait until tomorrow to find out how he got out of this one. Both Grandpa and I knew he would. "Always have faith in Alley Oop," Grandpa would say. "He's a resourceful one. He always has something up his sleeve. You could do worse than Alley Oop for a hero."

"I want a hero with ears," I said.

"Good point," Grandpa said. "Do you want me to fold you a hat from the comics page, Davy?"

"Yes, please, Grandpa."

Grandpa Homer could fold the most amazing hats from a page of the morning newspaper. He could fold boats, too, but I liked his hats best. I always liked wearing hats when I was a little boy.

"Do you want a hat like Emperor Napoleon Bonaparte?"

"Yes, I want one just like that." I didn't know who Emperor Napoleon Bonaparte was, but I loved the name. I was happy with my name, David Willson, but there was nothing special about it. Not when you heard it. When I told Grandpa that, he laughed.

"When you are older, Davy, you'll find out there is something special about our name, something that gives people fits. We spell our Willson differently. We put an extra 'L' in it, and that displeases many folks who think we are putting on airs. My brother Bert got so tired of it that he stopped spelling it with two 'Ls.'"

"I don't know how to spell anything except soap, because I heard it on the radio so many times. L-A-V-A," I said.

Again, Grandpa laughed. "That's not soap. That's a kind of soap. Lava."

While we were talking, he'd folded me my Napoleon hat. "Here's your hat, Davy." He placed it on my head. It fit me perfectly. It always did.

"How do you fold the hat so it always fits my head?"

"It's an old Masonic secret," Grandpa said. "I can't tell you."

"Or you'd have to kill me?"

"What? No. What are you talking about?"

"Nothing. Just something a mean man who lives in Grandma Alma's boarding house said to me."

"I'd like to give him a piece of my mind," Grandpa said.

"Otto. That's the man's name."

"He doesn't know how to talk right to people," Grandpa said.

"No, he doesn't."

"Well, I've got to go to work pretty soon." Grandpa got down his work jacket from an iron hook on the wall of the boxcar. He dug in a pocket and took out a small, thin, silver-and-black book. He sat back down at the kitchen table, opened up the little book, and wrote a couple of lines in it with a small stub of yellow pencil.

"What're you doing, Grandpa?"

"Just making a brief notation in my diary, Davy."

"Why do you do that, Grandpa?"

"I like to keep track of what I do each day."

"What did you write down this time?"

"I wrote down, 'Ate breakfast with Davy. Toast and eggs. Hen in a hole.'"

"Have you written about me before in your diary?"

"Sure." He thumbed through his diary. "See. On this page I wrote, 'Bob and Alice and Davy came on No. 2, 5-21-44.'"

"Number 2 is the train?"

"Right. Then on 5-22-44 I wrote, 'Alice caught 3 big Red Bellies at mouth of Thompson River. Bob caught 1 and I caught 1.' Here I wrote your address: 'Alice H. Willson, Route 5, Box 118, Riverside California. 5-22-44.'" He paged forward. "On 3-12-45, I wrote 'Got 1 letter from Iwo.'"

"When I grow up, I'm going to write in a diary, too, Grandpa, like you."

"It's a good habit to get into. You never know when you might need that information," he said.

I drank my coffee milk.

"Time for me to go off to work. Done with that?"

I nodded.

He took our cups, rinsed them out, then dumped his ashtray out into the stove, washed it out, and dried it. He put on his work jacket and his flat cap. "Don't ever sign up for the life of a working man, Davy. You can do better," Grandpa said.

"Okay, Grandpa. I won't."

HUCKLEBERRIES

"Davy, it looks like we'll be going huckleberrying after all," Grandpa Homer said.

Huckleberries were a big thing in Thompson Falls, Montana, and during World War II, they were more important than ever. It was a drab, worried time, perhaps even more for a four-year-old than for the sober, hard working adults who had responsibility for me. It was my father who was gone to be a Marine on Guam and Iwo Jima, gone to kill Japs. I understood that they might kill him, too.

Huckleberries were there now, ripe to be picked. Free for the taking. All you had to do was load the people and the huckleberry buckets and lunches and large jars of lemonade to drink, and drive out into the hills and pick buckets full of berries, every once in a while emptying the buckets into large baskets.

I loved huckleberrying. Even at four years old, I appreciated its festive aspects. I made no contribution; mostly I was just in the way while the adults picked. I understood that, too. Huckleberrying was little different from the rest of my life during World War II. There was no place for a little boy. I'd heard people ask Mom more than once why she hadn't waited until after the war to have me. "That would have made more sense," she was told.

I could see that.

But I loved huckleberries—the taste, the smell of them, and the pies and jellies and other treats that Grandma Katherine made from them. I also loved being out in the hills and woods and meadows. I loved the smell of the pine trees and the sounds of the birds all around. We'd see deer for sure.

With any luck, we might see bear.

When I told Grandpa Homer that, he said, "I hope not."

He told me that where we were going I might find arrowheads, as Indians used to hunt that area and they also gathered berries there. "We'll be on the edge of the area where Nigger Bill used to have his orchards and vineyards, too. It's mostly gone or overgrown now, but there are still old bottles you might find for your collection."

"Nigger Bill?"

"He was an old character in these parts in the 20's and 30's— an upstanding citizen who went crazy and ended up in the county home for the insane."

I must have looked worried.

"Don't worry. He's long gone. Besides, he was harmless. Worry about the bear, if you want to worry," Grandpa said.

"I want to see a bear."

"Not me. I've seen enough bear to last me. They like huckleberries as much as we do. They're gorging themselves with berries now, getting ready to hibernate for the winter. They have to eat a ton of berries to get ready for that."

"Will we hibernate, too?"

"No, we won't do that. We don't have enough sense to hibernate."

"Have you ever seen a bear hibernate?"

"Yes, just once. I was deer hunting up near the top of that hill." We were out in the driveway of the boxcar we lived in, and I was helping Grandpa load buckets in the trunk of his old Chevy. I looked up where he pointed.

Thompson Falls was located in a deep, narrow valley that sun didn't shine down into very long each day. He'd pointed at a very tall mountain. Idaho was on the other side, or so he had told me. "Where did you see the bear hibernate?" I asked.

"Well, I was deer hunting up there and I lost track of how late in the day it was. It started snowing, really hard. I looked for an overhang or a shallow cave for shelter, where I could build a fire and wait for the snow to wear itself out.

"Soon enough I found one. I gathered up some squawwood and pinecones and started a fire near the front of the overhang, but back out of the storm a bit. I had the fire going pretty good, so I took stock of my surroundings. I soon realized my shelter was more of a cave than I'd thought it was. I lit a branch like a torch and held it up near the ceiling. The ceiling had a wide golden streak in it. I got out my hunting knife and gouged out some of it.

"For once it wasn't iron pyrite, fools gold, but it was the real thing. I put the chips in a little malted milk bottle I always carried with me for samples in the pocket of my hunting coat, screwed the lid on tight and made plans to come back in the spring.

"Around then, I heard a noise in the back in the darkness of the cave. I lit another branch and held it up. What did I behold? You tell me, Davy."

"A hibernating bear!"

"Yes, the very same. But he was interrupting his long snooze to see what I was up to."

"What were you up to, Grandpa?"

"I was up to no good. Gold mining in his cave," Grandpa said.

"What did you do then?"

"I grabbed up my 3o.o6 and vamoosed out into the storm. Lucky for me, it was letting up."

"Why didn't you shoot the bear?"

"It was his cave. I was the interloper. He belonged there. I didn't."

"Did you ever go back there for more gold?"

"Yes, I did. At least I tried to."

"What did you find, Grandpa?"

"No cave. A huge landslide had obliterated the whole area," he said.

"Oblit..."

"Yes, obliterated. It was all gone."

"Do you think the bear got hurt?"

"No, I'm sure he did not. Bear have a sixth sense. He was long gone before the landslide."

"Maybe we'll see him when we're picking huckleberries," I said.

"I hope not. He was a very large brown bear," Grandpa said.

"Would you know him if you saw him again?"

"I would."

"How?"

"He had one normal ear and one ear that was mostly chewed off."

"Who would be crazy enough to chew on a bear's ear?"

"Another, bigger bear."

"Huh."

We drove up into the hills to what Grandpa Homer referred to as the Blue Slide Area. We went in a small convoy of cars. Mom and Grandma Katherine and Aunt Nellie Mae and Aunt Allie and Uncle Bruce and two neighbors—Phoebe and her husband; I forget his name. We drove through the area where Nigger Bill had had what he called the Orchard of the Lord, located on the Hill of the Lord. It was hard to see he'd ever been there. There were just a few old fruit trees and some overgrown terraces.

"Are there ghosts here?" I asked Grandpa Homer.

"People claim there are, but I never saw any. There used to be a lot of bear congregate here in the fall, to eat the apples and pears and plums off of Bill's trees and the fruit that collected on the ground. No ghosts, though."

* * *

We drove up to the area Grandpa and the others had staked out for the day of picking.

"Keep your eyes peeled for a bear, Davy. Rattlesnakes, too. If you see a bear, sit still and holler 'Bear!'"

"Okay, Grandpa. What will I do if I see a rattlesnake?"

"Don't sit still. Jump away and holler 'Snake.'"

"Okay, Grandpa, will that do it?"

"It'll do something."

Mom found a sandy area with some gravel, like a dried up creek bed, and told me to "sit tight." She said she'd find me some berries to eat.

I had a bucket of my own. I sat there for a long time, sorting through the sand and gravel for arrowheads. I found none. I did find a small agate. I got bored and decided to pick some berries. There was a big clump of huckleberry bushes a few feet away. I dumped the gravel out of my little bucket and wiped it out with the tail of my shirt.

I walked over to the bushes and started picking huckleberries. I could hear I was not alone in this patch of berries. I could hear somebody, or something, picking berries on the other side.

I slowly inched around the edge of the bushes. The noise stopped. I kept inching.

"BOO!"

Yikes! I just about came out of my skin.

It was Aunt Nellie Mae. "What would you have done if I'd been a big brown bear?" she asked.

"I would have hollered 'Bear!'" I said.

"Yes, that would be one way to deal with a bear. Do you want some berries?"

"Yes, please," I said.

She poured some into my little bucket. I went back to my gravelly area and sat there until lunchtime, eating berries. I got pretty stained.   I gobbled them all down. We all got together by the cars and ate lunch together—bologna sandwiches.

After lunch we picked more berries.

We didn't see a bear on that huckleberry adventure. I was disappointed.

Nobody else was.

GRANDPA'S SISTER

We'd been gone all day up Vermillion Creek, picking huckleberries. I was bothered by an itchy bug bite. "Grandpa, I got a bug stuck on me. Can you fix it?"

"Bring it on over here, and I'll take a look at it, Davy." Grandpa Homer was sitting at the kitchen table in the boxcar we lived in, drinking a cup of coffee and smoking a cigarette.

I went over to the table and showed him my arm.

"You got a tick, Davy. A woodtick. But you caught him early. We'll back him out of there in a jiffy and get rid of him." Grandpa puffed hard on his Camel and brought it down close to the woodtick. I could feel the heat of the cigarette on my arm. The tiny black tick scrambled out of my arm, and Grandpa snatched him up between thumb and forefinger and crushed him. Blood appeared on Grandpa's thumb. "That's the end of him," Grandpa said.

"Now what?" I asked.

"We'll wash out the bite with some rubbing alcohol, and Bob's your uncle." He got up and went to the bathroom and brought back a bottle of alcohol and a ball of cotton, and scrubbed the bite hard. The alcohol stung a little bit.

"You gotta be careful with tick bites, Davy," he said.

"Why? Are they worse than mosquito bites?"

"They can be. My sister Marian died from a tick bite."

"She did? I didn't know you had a sister."

"I did have a sister. Marian, until she died of Rocky Mountain Spotted Fever. That was one of the saddest days in my life," Grandpa said.

"Not the saddest?"

"No, not the saddest."

"I don't think I want to hear about the saddest day," I said.

"Maybe someday I'll tell you," he said.

"Okay," I said. "Do you have a picture of your sister?"

"I do have a picture—more than one. Let me see if I can find one." Grandpa got up from his chair. He put out his cigarette in the ashtray on the table.

The smoke made my eyes water. I liked the smell.

Grandpa went over to the old trunk they stored stuff in. He lifted the lid and rummaged around in the trunk. This was the same trunk where he kept the shoebox full of picture postcards of his Army days. "Oh, here it is," he said. He stood with his back to me for a couple of minutes. He then turned around, wiped his eyes with his sleeve and came back over to the table where I waited for him.

He put the photo down on the table and sat down. He lit another cigarette. Took a sip of cold coffee.

I looked at the picture. There were three kids in it.

"That's Marian there." He pointed at the girl on the left of the picture.

"Who's that other little girl, on the big chair?"

Grandpa laughed. "That's me, Davy. That's how they dressed little boys in the 1880's. I was born in 1887. So I was about two in that photograph. The baby of the family. Four brothers and one sister, who we all cherished and looked out for. But to no avail. A tiny bite from a tiny bug took her away from us forever. There's a lesson in that," he said. "I wish I knew what it was."

"Don't get bit by a bug," I said.

"Life consists of getting bug bites. No way to avoid them."

"Who is the big boy on your other side?"

"That's my brother Bert—Herbert," Grandpa said.

"His ears really stick out."

"Yes, those ears of his were the bane of his life. People would ask him, 'Who left the barn doors open?'"

"Your ears don't stick out. Marian's don't either," I said.

"No, they don't."

"How come you got to sit on that fancy chair and your brother and sister had to stand up?"

"They were the big kids. I was the baby."

"What's that stuff on the ground, Grandpa?"

"That's hay. You've got sharp eyes."

"Hay?"

"Yes, hay. This photo was not taken in a city studio. An itinerant photographer traveled from farm to farm in his old jalopy with a fancy camera on a tripod, a rolled-up backdrop and that fancy chair, too. And he took pictures."

"Who wanted their pictures took?"

"Our mother loved photographs of her family. When the chance came by, she took advantage. Dad was seldom around so there are no pictures of him on that farm in Lo Lo."

"What's that in your lap, Grandpa?"

"That's my ball. I carried it everywhere. My dad gave it to me."

"Did it bounce?"

"Not much. It did roll a bit."

"Your sister was a cute girl," I said.

"All us Willsons were handsome," Grandpa said.

"Bert?"

"Well, he was no great shakes in the looks department, but God, how he could fiddle."

"Is he dead, too?"

"Yes, he died last year in Idaho. His Spanish American War time finally caught up with him."

"Did Marian live to grow up?"

"She did. She died over forty years ago, but she was grown up. And married. With a little baby boy, Gordon."

"Gordon? I met him," I said.

"Yes, you did. That time we all went to Missoula and out to Lo Lo, to his ranch."

"He lost his mom a long time ago," I said.

"Yes, it was 1903. Marian was eighteen years old. She got bit on April fifteenth. She died in less than two weeks. In those days there was nothing could be done for her. Just watch her die. She was still nursing baby Gordon, but the doctors were afraid that the poison in her body might sicken him, so he had to be given a bottle. During that time, Marian's husband Frank almost went crazy. Trying to care for Gordon and dealing with Marian's suffering. If my mother hadn't been living with them, I don't know what Frank would have done. That's your Great Grandma. She cared for Marian until she died, then she mothered Gordon. Hard, hard times, Davy."

"When are the easy times, Grandpa?"

Grandpa was quiet for a long time. He puffed on his cigarette. He got up and went to the stove and brought back the blue-and-white-speckled coffee pot, using an old potholder. He poured himself some coffee. "Do you want a touch with some milk, Davy?"

"No, thanks, Grandpa."

"To answer your question, Davy, there are no easy times. That's why we have to be able to take pleasure in small things, like a cigarette or a cup of coffee. It would be better if you never got enslaved by those things, but they got into my nature in the Army, and never got back out again."

"Do you have a picture of your sister with baby Gordon?"

"Only the one." Grandpa went back to the trunk and rattled around and came back with the picture. "Here it is." He placed it carefully on the kitchen table.

"When was that taken?"

Grandpa picked up the photo. Showed me the handwriting on the back, read it to me. "'This is myself and Baby Gordon, taken Nov. 24th 1902.' It's like a voice from beyond the grave."

Marian was standing in front of a farmhouse, holding a tiny baby.

"Were they cold?"

"Yes, they were. November in Lo Lo. That's why Baby Gordon is swaddled up so all you can see is his eyes."

"What color were his eyes?"

"Well, they were, and still are, blue. Like most Willsons'."

"Not mine," I said.

"No, not yours."

"How come none of you are smiling in the fancy chair photo?"

"I suspect there wasn't anything much to smile about that day," Grandpa said.

"My mom always tells me to smile when my picture is being taken."

"I've heard her do that. But you don't smile. You are a sober little citizen."

"I guess so."

"Plenty to be sober about," Grandpa said.

"That's a sad story about Marian, Grandpa," I said.

"Yes, most stories are sad, Davy. That's the way life is. You work hard, do the best you can and then you die."

"I do the best I can, Grandpa. Who would take care of me if my mom died?"

"Probably Aunt Nellie Mae would. Unless you ended up in Seattle."

"I'd rather be here with you, Grandpa."

"I'm not long for this world, Davy. You'd do better with N'Mae and Uncle Bob. But your mom is tough. Marian wasn't tough. And medicine was primitive then. Now a woodtick won't kill you. Of course, there's polio. I worry myself sick about that."

"Polio?"

"Yes, that's a scourge here in the west."

"Could I get polio?"

"Yes, you could."

"How?"

"We're not sure, but probably from water. Water-borne diseases are killers," Grandpa said.

"I don't much like swimming anyhow. I don't like getting cold and wet all over."

"Mostly polio cripples people or kills them outright. I have nightmares about that happening."

"Now I'll have them, too."

"There's lots to be worried sick about, Davy. I've spent my whole life worrying. But worry didn't keep Marian alive. Worry doesn't." Grandpa got up and put the pictures back in the old trunk.

The door opened: Mom and Grandma and Aunt Nellie Mae, home from the store with groceries. "What are you two up to?"

"Just talking," I said.

"About what?" Nellie Mae asked.

"Polio," I said. "And I had a tick bite that Grandpa fixed."

"God Almighty!" Grandma said.

"Let's use those huckleberries and make a pie," Mom said.

So that's what we did.

Well, Grandpa and I didn't. I wanted to help roll out the piecrust, so I stood on a chair at the counter and made an effort, but not much of one. Then I helped Grandpa get wood for the stove. We stoked up the fire and got out of the way. The women made us dinner and also huckleberry pie, which we ate for dessert.

Grandma used bear lard to make the crust. "That's what makes it so flakey," she said.

They'd even brought home ice cream for the pie. We ate it all up, as it would just melt otherwise.

It was hard to believe that morning the huckleberries had been on their bushes up Vermillion Creek, waiting for the bear to eat them. Now they were in our stomachs, along with our dinner of fried chicken, mashed potatoes, and green beans with bacon.

When I said this to Grandpa, he said, "That's how life works, Davy. If we didn't get those berries, and make pie out of them, the bear would eat them. Next season there'll be more berries on those bushes."

"Unless there's another fire that burns through there," Nellie Mae said.

"Always looking on the bright side," my mother said.

"Anyone want the last piece of pie?" Grandma asked.

"I'll take it," Grandpa said. "Hate to see it go to waste. Want a corner of it, Davy?"

"Okay, Grandpa."

We ate the last piece of pie at the table as the women cleaned up the kitchen. Grandpa smoked a cigarette and drank another cup of coffee. "Good pie, eh, Davy?"

"Yes, it is Grandpa." And it was.

The best pie I ever ate in my life.

GRANDPA IN THE ARMY

Grandpa Homer and I sat at the kitchen table in our boxcar home in Thompson Falls, Montana. He had his shoebox of photo postcards spread out on the tabletop. "When I went into the Army in 1910, I was twenty years older than you are right now. Same age as Bob in the Marines," he said.

"Why didn't Daddy go into the Army like you did?"

"He thought he'd be smart and end up in the Navy as a pilot. He outsmarted himself. Now he's a Marine Corps rifleman, infantry, like I was in the Army. They didn't need pilots. They needed a man to carry a rifle and shoot that rifle at the enemy. So that's what he's doing."

"Did you do that in the Philippines?"

"Not exactly," Grandpa said. "What did I do? Mostly, I remember how hot it seemed to me there. I grew up in Montana, so the heat just about killed me at first. Our uniforms seemed hot enough at Fort Missoula, but at Camp Keithley in Mindanao, near Zamboanga, they were pure itchy suffering, especially on one of those long, uphill forced marches the 6th Infantry so loved to keep us busy with."

"What did you do, Grandpa?"

"I marched. One step at a time. If you ever have to go for to be a soldier, avoid being a foot soldier. Avoid the infantry. You aren't much of a walker anyhow. By the time you might be a soldier, the cavalry—that's horse soldiers—will be gone. There will be jeeps and trucks that take the place of horses and mules. That's the ticket, the cavalry. Walking all those miles, always uphill, with tropical bugs in close attendance—you don't want that, Davy."

"No, I don't. I don't like mosquitoes," I said.

"Well, then steer clear of the hot climate countries. Mosquitos are in their element there. And white men are not. Malaria is a threat there. Montana is God's country. In the Philippines, the only seasons are hot and wet, or hotter and wetter."

"How long were you in the Philippines, in the Army?"

"Fifteen months. But it seemed like fifteen years."

"Did you have adventures there? Did you have battles with the people there?"

"No battles. It wasn't that kind of a war. Not by the time I got there," Grandpa said.

"What kind was it?"

"It's hard for me to tell you. I didn't know what kind of a war it was when I was in the middle of it. Mostly we did the same things, the same sorts of Army routines in the Philippines that we'd done at Fort Missoula. Standing guard duty, marching, KP duty, endless cleaning of the barracks to impossibly high standards, the usual Army BS. Except it was a lot hotter in the Philippines, and the bugs were a lot bigger. There had been battles before I got there, but that part of the war was mostly over except for occasional skirmishes, and the Moros—the Moslem warriors—who'd pop up when you least expected them to. Just the thought of those Moros terrified us. Most of us were ordinary boys from small towns and farms, in a land that was so alien we did not know which end was up."

"Had you been a farmer before you went into the Army?"

"Nope. I hated farming. I'd been working as a waiter in the restaurant of the Missoula Hotel. I loved getting the tips and being clean and dressed up. And they gave us one big meal a day, free, all we could eat. I loved that part of it. But that job was not going anywhere. My brothers had been in the Army, so I decided to try that. The Spanish American War was long over, but they needed men to keep the Moros in line, so I figured, why not me? 'Three hots and a cot.' My brothers kept telling me that. Meals and a place to sleep. And that scratchy uniform I mentioned.

"When my dad found out I'd joined the Army, he did everything he could think of to get me out, but it was too late. Besides, I wanted to go. He told me, 'You'll be sorry.' Dad wrote a letter to my mother in which he said enough Willson boys had served their country in uniform. It was time for others to sign up and march away."

"Did your dad fight in the Army?"

"He was in the Civil War. Down south as a teenager. He didn't talk about it much. He did say he'd guarded prisoners. That's about all he ever said. He enlisted to get the signing bonus. Times was hard and his family needed the money. Times were never good for the Willsons."

"Tell me an Army adventure, Grandpa."

"Well, as you can tell from some of these picture postcards, some of the stories aren't for the ears of little boys." Grandpa Homer shuffled the postcards that showed men, "Filipinos or Moros," he called them, lying dead in ditches. "The ditches were full of them, dead as mackerels, but there were always a lot more where those came from. In Asia, there's an endless supply of dusky warriors armed with long, sharp knives, ready and willing to defeat armies of white men who seek to tame them and their wild native ways. Some of those white men ended up dead in ditches themselves, but no photo postcards were made of them."

"Why do we pester them? The Moros? Couldn't we leave them be?"

"That's the hundred dollar question, Davy. Me and the other privates asked that question, but got no answer. I even asked the world-famous General Black Jack Pershing that question one time, but got back only a blank stare. I'd been assigned to serve him his dessert course at a banquet he was the guest of honor at. He was then the military commander of Moro Province, in which Camp Keithley was located."

"You were in Camp Keithley," I said.

"Yes, I was assigned there for most of my time in the Philippines. That was a time ago, and as a private, those kinds of thoughts and questions were not encouraged. Maybe they still aren't. Pershing was a fair enough man, but he seemed pretty full of himself. That's how all officers seemed to me, a private from Montana. I was easily dismissed as just another cowboy who'd joined the Army to get away from the cows. That was part of it, but I'd never been a cowboy."

"Was Black Jack a black man?'"

"What? No. No, Black Jack Pershing was a white man who had commanded Buffalo soldiers, who were black men. Negroes, we call them now. Because General Pershing was the guest of honor for dinner at Camp Keithley, it was quite a meal we served him. Many courses. All served by soldiers wearing white gloves. I served him his dessert: apple pie made from dried apples and abutted by a slab of cheddar cheese. I put down the dessert and cheese in front of him and asked, "Why do we pester the Moros so? Why don't we just leave them be and go home?"

"Then what happened, Grandpa?"

"General Pershing gave me the coldest stare I'd ever received. He looked me up and down, as if measuring me for my casket. 'Private, you need a haircut,' Black Jack Pershing told me, in his general's voice.

"'Yes, sir,' I said.

"'When's the last time you got a haircut?'

"'This morning, Sir,' I said.

"'The tropics make a soldier's hair grow. Keep that in mind in the future.'

"'Yes, sir. Thank you sir,' I said."

"Are there any photo postcards of you with Black Jack?'"

"No, that sort of thing did not happen. You'll notice that all of the many photo postcards in this box show me with my buddies, other privates and one corporal and one sergeant. What were called 'enlisted men.' Generals did not get their pictures taken with privates. Not unless the private was holding his horse. I never held the general's horse. All I ever did was serve him apple pie and cheese. And ask him the question he ignored."

"Did you get apple pie and cheese, too, Grandpa?"

"I did. Later, in the kitchen. I got a plate with a big slab of hot apple pie and cheddar cheese melted on the top of it, and a big Army mug of hot black coffee to wash all of it down. One of the perks of doing kitchen duty," Grandpa said.

"What did you think of General Pershing?"

"Well, he really put the hurt on the Moros. He was a great general. I think he'd have been a chilly friend or father, but it's hard to know. I talked to one of his sergeants who was along with him on this visit to Camp Keithley. He ate with me in the kitchen. He said that Black Jack was an okay boss. Lenient with the sergeant's problems with drink. Even forgiving. He was fair to me. I know that."

"So that was your day then, Grandpa?"

"Not quite, Davy. In the Army, especially if you are stationed in Asia, you never dare to let down your guard. That night when we were asleep in the barracks, one of us got his throat cut from ear to ear. When reveille sounded in the morning, he did not hear it or answer its call. The doc figured he'd got his throat cut sometime in the wee hours. Between midnight and three a.m."

"What did you think when you found him?"

"I was glad it wasn't me. Honestly, we all were. It could have been any one of us."

"Why him?"

"We all asked that question. His bunk was closest to a door. The barracks guard must have been at the other end. The Moro was in and out, quiet as a shadow. At least he didn't take Old Billy's head with him. Sometimes they did that."

"What would they do with a soldier's head?"

"Some of the Moros are headhunters and cannibals, or maybe they would want a trophy. We'll never know."

"Did they catch the Moro?"

"It could have been any one of thousands. Could have been one who worked at Camp Keithley, doing menial tasks we didn't do. Cleaning the latrines and the stables. Could have been the one who cut my hair and shaved me that morning. You never knew."

"You couldn't trust them?"

"Nope, you couldn't. They hated us. Wanted us out of their country. I don't blame them for that. But I still have nightmares about that night. I still wake up at night thinking I heard a Moro creeping into my bedroom to cut my throat."

"Not in Montana."

"No. Not in Montana. But once fear is inside of you, it stays there, and comes out at night."

"I have bad dreams lots of nights."

"I know you do," Grandpa said.

"I didn't know grownups had nightmares."

"They do. Especially if they've been to war."

"Will my dad have nightmares about Japs when he gets back home?"

"I suspect he will. We'll have to be patient with him when he returns."

"I'll just be glad to have my dad back."

"Me, too," Grandpa said.

"Let's look at the rest of the postcards tomorrow, Grandpa," I said.

"Good idea, Davy." Grandpa shuffled the photo postcards together and returned them to the shoebox. "Someday these will be yours to care for, Davy. Promise to take good care of them. We don't want to ever forget where we've been. Or what we've done."

"I promise, Grandpa. Cross my heart," I said.

GRANDPA'S BROTHERS

"You said your dad didn't want you to go into the Army. That the Willsons had done enough," I said to Grandpa Homer.

We were sitting at the kitchen table on a Sunday morning. We were drinking mugs of coffee, mine fixed special for a four-year-old boy, mostly milk; Grandpa's "so strong you could stand a spoon up in it," according to him. He also said you couldn't leave a spoon in it too long, or the spoon would melt. Grandpa was smoking a cigarette that he rolled himself. He said that, at the end of the month, that was all he could afford. "We don't live in a boxcar out of choice," he said.

My mom, Aunt Nellie Mae, and Grandma Katherine were off somewhere, perhaps out to Whitepine to clean up family graves.

"Two of my brothers served in the Spanish American War," Grandpa said. "Bert never got out of Georgia due to the fever. But brother Frank made it to Cuba with Teddy Roosevelt, and he went up Kettle Hill with him, somehow dodging Mauser bullets. Frank was a great horseman, a real cowboy, a hand-picked Rough Rider, but there were no horses for the men, only for some officers."

"Where were the rest of the horses, Grandpa?"

"I'm not sure. Maybe they didn't make it off of the ships. Maybe they drowned trying to swim ashore."

"I hope they didn't drown. What happened to Frank after he went up that hill with Teddy?"

"Well, everything since then was downhill for Frank. Hard to top that experience with Teddy. Someday you'll study that event in school, and you'll find out what happened to the horses. I hope you will."

"Did you study it in school, Grandpa?"

"I never really went to school, Davy," he said. "A couple of years in Lo Lo. That's about it. My mother was a schoolteacher. She had the certificates, so she taught us at home. A couple of hours a day. Mostly she focused on the 3 R's—reading, writing and 'rithmetic. She was a bearcat for penmanship."

"Which one were you good at?"

"All of 'em. I loved all of 'em. My brothers did, too, except for Tracy. He was the one they used to call a 'hell raiser' or a 'bad seed.' Dr. Freud put an end to those names. Tracy could not sit still at school."

"Dr. Freud?"

"You'll study him in school, too, Davy, one day."

"What happened to Tracy?'

"Nothing good. But he had serious adventures. He joined Coxey's Army, met Jack London, who wrote a book, *Call of the Wild*, that you'll read one day. He died young in Rawlins, Wyoming, shot dead by a deputy sheriff who thought Tracy was paying undo attention to his young wife."

"Was Tracy doing that?"

"Knowing Tracy, he was. Like all Willson men, he was a good-looking devil, and he had no idea when or how to keep his mouth shut. Our father took the train to Rawlins to find out what happened to him. He found out plenty—none of it good. I think Tracy's death in Rawlins is what provoked Dad to write that last letter he wrote to

Mom from the Tekoa Hotel. Dad didn't want to lose another son — in my case, the baby of the family. I was many years younger than Bert and Frank and my other older brother, Ed. Bert and Frank were the Spanish American War veterans who had dodged that bullet. Well, they survived their war. Ed dodged the whole thing by keeping his head down and watching the rear end of a horse plowing his farmland. "

"What did your dad find out about Tracy when he went to Wyoming?"

"He found out that Tracy died in a milkhouse on the ranch he was working as a ranch hand on. He was drinking a dipperful of cool milk, one of Tracy's many weaknesses. He was just a big overgrown boy. He never grew up. He didn't get the chance to."

"What's a milkhouse, Grandpa?"

"This milkhouse was built of fieldstone, down into the ground, around an artesian spring that produced ice cold water. They'd built it so it was down a few stairs, and the milk was stored in big metal cans and kept very cold there until needed. Tracy was down in the milkhouse, in the shadows, holding that metal dipper up to his mouth, when the deputy sheriff — who'd been told where to find Tracy — descended the steps stealthily and shot Tracy in the head with his pistol."

"Tracy didn't even see the deputy coming?"

"Probably not. He had the dipper up to his mouth, and he was turned away from the stairs, according to the reports."

"That doesn't seem fair," I said.

"There's a lesson in that, Davy — about life. The deputy claimed he thought Tracy was armed and about to take a shot at him. He thought the dipper was a gun. So he testified at the hearing. Tracy had no firearm on him. Only that metal milk dipper. He died with milk and blood all mixed down his face. He took a few days to die. But he was dead and buried by the time our family was notified." Grandpa tapped the ash off his cigarette into his ashtray. "Dad went right down to seek satisfaction but none was obtained. Tracy had been witnessed calling the deputy sheriff an SOB in a public place—a bar. When Tracy drank, he'd say anything to anybody. There's a lesson in that, too, Davy."

"I don't ever say much, Grandpa."

"I've noticed. Not a bad way to be, Davy. Tracy was a blowhard and a devil with the women. I'm surprised he lived as long as he did in Wyoming. I thought he'd get hanged when he joined Coxey's Army."

"What was Coxey's Army?"

"Davy, that's a long history lecture. Not for us here at the kitchen table." He leaned back. "Suffice it to say it was another lost cause— seeking fair wages and justice for the working man. Heed me, Davy: don't ever become a working man, a wage slave, and don't ever join the Army."

"Okay, Grandpa."

"I hope times won't be so hard for you like they were for my older brothers, Bert and Frank. They weren't so much patriots raring to Remember the Maine, and to punish the perfidy of the Spanish, as they were sick of farm work and their stomachs seeking to digest their backbones out of hunger. You follow me, Davy?"

"I try to, Grandpa," I said.

"You are a good boy, Davy. To sit with me, keep an old man company as I blather on about long-gone times and hard times. Sometimes I just talk to hear the sound of my own voice, to reassure myself that I still can draw breath, but I do like it when you sit there and listen to me."

"I always listen, Grandpa. Later sometimes I figure it out."

"I'm sure you do, Davy. You are a smart little boy," he said. "Smarter than folks take you for. You keep your own counsel. Not a bad thing."

"How did Bert and Frank do after their war?"

"Well, Bert got typhoid fever in Florida, and his health was ruined for the rest of his life. His stories of the suffering he endured in that hospital gave me nightmares. Somehow he survived it, but that fever stove him in, so he could never properly catch his breath. He got a small pension, not enough to make a difference. He got burned out in the 1910 Fire. Disaster followed him," he said. "He lost just about everything. He somehow managed to get out of it with his life, but the house he'd not even finished building burned. It wasn't much of a house, but it was all he had to live in while he farmed those few miserable acres he'd homesteaded. Trying to feed his family, mostly rutabagas, I figure. They lived poor—hand-to-mouth."

"Did Frank farm, too?"

"Nope, Frank hated anything like farming. He kept getting out of the Army, and then trying and failing to make it on Civvy Street. Then he'd go back into the Army. He served several hitches, and died in an old soldiers' home in Sawtelle, California. His personal effects were mostly pawn tickets and oil stocks. And an old typewriter. He was writing his memoirs. His claim to fame all his life was that he'd gone up Kettle Hill with Teddy Roosevelt. He learned that lesson from our dad. How to be a professional old soldier.

"Our father spent his whole life coasting on his time in the Army in the Civil War. He was the post master in Brocksburg, Nebraska, mostly because he was a Civil War veteran and he was literate. That's about all it took in those days. My dad drifted all over the west, settled down long enough to talk his way into one old soldiers' home after the other. Even though he never lived long in Oregon, he got into an old soldiers' home there. My pop had a silver tongue. He could talk himself into just about anything, and sometimes out, too."

"I wish I could have met him."

"You missed him by a mile, Davy. My pop hated hard work, especially farming, so my mom raised us on that worthless farm in Lo Lo, Montana. She got the occasional letter from him, describing his next scheme for striking it rich. He always figured there was large quantities of money just around the next bend. He wrote that last letter from Tekoa, Washington. We never heard from him again.

"I went down there, looking for him, so he could show up for my wedding to Katherine Haase. I looked in Tekoa, because that was the last place we had evidence that he'd been. When I wrote the U. S. Government about him, they wrote me a letter saying that his last pension check for his Civil War service disability had sat there in the Tekoa Post Office, eternally unclaimed.

"I knew when I got that letter that my pop had to be dead. No Willson with the breath of life left in him would leave a government check unclaimed at the Post Office."

"Were you sad?"

"Sure, but I'd already figured out that Pop must have come to the end of the line. His last letter said he was going to travel to Portland, Oregon, to visit the Lawrences there, and then book passage on a coaster to California.

"I contacted the Lawrences, and they said they'd not seen hide nor hair of him during that time. Pop and Brother Bert had gotten entangled with some gamblers in Idaho, just before Pop wrote that Tekoa letter. Bert had cheated at the card game, and won big. He'd skedaddled on back to Montana then, but Pop had stayed in Tekoa.

"I figured the gamblers had caught up with pop and settled the score. Tekoa in those days was a rough town to get on the wrong side of folks in. Just like Rawlins was for Tracy. Railroad men, miners, grifters. They made Tekoa a rough town."

"Tekoa is a funny name, Grandpa. What does it mean?"

"It's probably some old Indian word, but I don't know what it means. Or maybe it's from the Bible. Anyhow, I figure Pop never got out of Tekoa alive—not far, anyhow. At first I'd hoped he'd caught that coaster that winter, but those coasters were notorious for being leaky old tubs, and going down with all on board in a storm. But I rejected that theory. I think his old bones molder in some remote ditch not far from Tekoa. It breaks my heart that he's not buried in the Missoula Cemetery with a Civil War marker over his bones. But

I've given up on that happening. Sometimes you have to let things go, Davy, just let 'em go. At least I know where Frank and Bert are buried."

"Where's your brother Tracy buried?"

"He's in a pauper's grave in Rawlins. I always wanted to have him disinterred and reburied next to our mother. To bring him back home one last time. Not going to happen. When you live your life out working for the Northern Pacific Railroad, and you live in a box-car, a grand scheme like that is always going to fail for lack of funds.

"Anyway, I decided early on I would not go the way of my father and brothers," Grandpa said. "I set my mind to get a job, stick with it through thick and thin, and take my pension at the end, were I lucky enough to live so long. And that's what I am doing. I hate the NPRR, but it's not like I ever got a better offer. So I'll be a signal maintainer until I retire or die."

He pushed himself away from the table. "Let's fry up some eggs. All this rambling and recollecting has made me hungry. How about you, Davy?"

"I'm hungry, too, Grandpa," I said.

"You crack 'em and I'll fry 'em up. How does that sound?"

"Sounds good, Grandpa. Then can we read Alley Oop?"

"You betcha."

SMOKE CHASER

"You asked me if I'd ever been a cowboy," Grandpa Homer said. "That was about the only low-paid, unskilled job I never had. I was a private in the Army, a copper miner in Butte, a farmer, a gandy-dancer, and I chased smoke for the U. S. Forest Service, which is about as close as I made it to being a cowboy."

We were drinking our morning coffee at the kitchen table in the boxcar we lived in during World War II. Well, he was drinking a mug of coffee; I was drinking a mug of mostly milk with a splash of coffee in it. "To put hair on your chest," Grandpa said.

"What was close about chasing smoke to being a cowboy? And what was chasing smoke?"

"Chasing smoke was me on a horse, my own horse, riding up and down wild canyons looking for smoke. Because where there's smoke, there's fire, more often than not. Or at least sometimes."

"Why would there be fire in the canyons?"

"After a thunder and lightning storm in the summer, often times there'd be smoke in some remote canyon," Grandpa said. "And I rode through all of 'em, and I seen just about everything one time or another."

"Like what, Grandpa?"

"I even saw a mangy old buffalo one time. He must've been somebody's pet buff that strayed off. He wasn't doing well. I could count his every rib. I expect not too long after, he was a meal for some coyotes."

"Couldn't you help him?"

"He was too big and evil-tempered for me to do anything but try to dodge him," Grandpa said. "Another time, I run across a big old red longhorn steer. Those horns of his were not built for those tight canyons choked with underbrush. He needed to be in Texas in the wide-open spaces. I couldn't do anything for him either.

"I saw lots of bear, of course. I gave them a wide berth. My horse, Old Sally, would get to snorting and acting skittish as soon as she caught scent of a bear. And I don't blame her none."

"How come you were doing that job?" I asked.

"Well, I had just married your grandma, and I'd quit the copper mines in Butte, and I hadn't yet been able to get on with the Northern Pacific Railroad, so I took that job with the Forest Service. It was 1914 and times was hard then. I was lucky to get that job. The only reason I got it was I had a horse, and I was willing to ride up and down all those canyons. It wasn't a picnic, but mostly it wasn't boring either, like going up and down the same set of railroad tracks, year after year." He took a swallow of his coffee. "Don't ever take a job where you have to do the same thing year after year, especially if you have a mean-spirited, cantankerous boss like mine, who is impossible to please—a nit-picking SOB, if ever there was one."

"Okay, Grandpa," I said.

"Your grandma and I were newly-weds, and lived in an old log cabin with a big front porch up above the Whitepine Creek Bridge. That's where we lived the whole year I rode for the Forest Service, chasing smoke. I rode from home to Thompson Point, which rose high over the old Meadows Ranch on Little Beaver Creek. I rode down Eley Gulch to where it ended at Ed Thompson's ranch," he said. "Eley was the man who set up a sawmill there while he logged off all the hills around there. I'd ride down Foote Gulch, which was below Larch Point in the Big Beaver Creek area. I rode all of 'em: Anderson Gulch, Haines Gulch, Miller Gulch, Readers Gulch, Grays Gulch—one gulch after the other. I knew them all like the back of my hand."

He showed me the back of his reddened, gnarled old hand—blue-veined and so crippled he could not make a proper fist.

"Did the Beaver creeks have lots of beavers?"

Grandpa laughed. "You have a keen ear, Davy. Yes, there were beaver aplenty. Those beaver were terrible pests. They loved that area, as there were lots of the kinds of trees they liked to build their dams out of. The people who lived near Little Beaver Creek and Big Beaver Creek were driven to distraction by those pesky beaver. Every winter the farmers would put out traps, but no matter how many they caught—and they caught plenty—there were always more beaver. The survivors built their dams and flooded the land. The beaver were none too particular about using trees that the farmers would have liked for other purposes."

"So the beavers won?"

"Well, they had no quit in them. They did what they were designed to do. And they did it well. They must have worked at night, and tucked themselves away in their dens during the day. I guess they were what biologists call 'nocturnal.' The farmers were not nocturnal. They worked hard all day long farming and needed to sleep at night. It was a losing battle for the farmers.

"But to be fair to the beaver, they were there first. They've been on that same land since time began. They are focused on building dams and flooding the meadows, making their dens, having their kits, living their lives. You gotta admire their tenacity."

He leaned forward over his coffee cup. "Where was I, Davy, before the beaver reared their toothy little heads?"

"Gulches, lots of gulches, chasing smoke."

"I only did that job, and all the other terrible jobs I had, because a man has to support his family and pay the mortgage if he owns a house. This is a boxcar we live in, but the railroad supplies it to the signal maintainer free, sort of. No mortgage. You'll never live in a boxcar, Davy. Your life will be better than that."

"I hope so, Grandpa."

"I've been living in boxcars or other similar cheap housing right by the railroad tracks since I got hired on by the NPRR. It's the only way a family man can afford to work for the railroad, at least at my low level as a signal maintainer—free housing, and a big garden full of vegetables, and a rented locker full of venison, elk, and bear steaks and chops, wrapped in brown waxed paper. Money always tight. And you work even if you are sick. You can stay home if you are sick, but if you do, you forfeit your pay. That's how the plutocrats have it fixed against the little guy, the ordinary working stiff—which I am and always have been and always will be. Where were we?"

"Riding Old Sally, chasing smoke," I said.

"Right. I rode up and down those canyons, gullies, gulches, ravines, and arroyos, chasing smoke," Grandpa Homer said.

"Did you find some?"

"I did. I wasn't supposed to fight fires myself, but I carried an entrenching tool, a canvas bucket, and an Army blanket, rolled up behind my saddle. Just in case. I would spot smoke, and by the time I got to it, the fire had burned itself out, or nearly so. A tall snag struck by lightning. A small grass fire caused by a spark from God knows what. The grass burned to the edge of a nearly dry creek and then sputtered out. I'd dip up some water with the canvas bucket and toss water here and there, or I'd soak the blanket in the muddy water left in the bottom of the creek, or use the shovel to dig up some muddy sand to throw on the smoldering grass. Just to feel like I was earning my two dollars a day."

"Did you ever find a fire you couldn't handle?"

"Oh, yes, once I did."

"What did you do then?"

"I followed U. S. Forest Service Procedure. When they hired me, I had to attend an indoctrination class in Missoula taught by a big, bald Forest Service muckety-muck, who I suspect had never put out a fire in his life. Except to maybe blow out candles on his birthday cake. He had the prettiest, softest, whitest hands I ever saw on a man. He probably had an assistant to scratch his butt for him. Anyhow, he spent a full day boring a room full of roughnecks like me. Well, there were a couple of state college boys who'd flunked out for pulling frat pranks. Everyone in the room, including the college boys, knew more about smoke and fire than our august instructor.

"We also got a U. S. Forest Service procedures manual. It read, 'Upon spotting smoke plumes, your duty is to investigate the source of the fire, its extent and duration. Then return to your office duty station, use the telephone to call the Forest Service Main Office, and give them the details of the fire—accurate location, size of fire and access points.'"

"Then what happened, Grandpa?"

"Next, a crew of men would be mobilized from the public places in the nearby towns, and they were transported out to fight the fire. Actually, what happened is that drunks and idlers from bars and taverns would be dragooned with offers of easy money and threats of jail to put out the fire."

"And that was that?"

"Ideally, that was that," Grandpa said.

"Did things ever go wrong?"

"Funny you'd ask that, Davy," Grandpa said. "One time, I was riding those tick-infested gulches on a hot July day—it felt like it was over 100 degrees in those gulches where all the trees had been burned off in the 1910 Fire. Remember, this was only four years later. Just tall burned-out snags stood, and they offered no shade. I was dripping with sweat, so I'd stopped for lunch when I ran across an old pine tree the fire had jumped over. There was a little creek nearby, so Old Sally could get a drink of water and eat some grass and watercress that grew down its banks. I sat on a log and ate my lunch, and watched green dragonflies dance and dart along the surface of the creek."

"What was your lunch that day?"

"I had a bologna sandwich with lots of yellow mustard, the way I like it. I'd added some watercress to it for some peppery crunch. I think Grandma had stuck in a couple of cookies, too."

"Then what happened?"

"Well, Old Sally started snorting and tossing her head. I figured she'd smelled a bear that was coming down to drink at the creek and eat some berries. This was real bear country. So I stood up and took a gander around.

"Sure enough, I spotted a big brown bear snuffling along the way they do. Following along behind her was not one, but two yearling cubs. Big enough to do real damage. I figured lunchtime was over. I'd tied Old Sally to a small bush, but she was tossing her head pretty high, and threatening to pull that little bush out by its roots. So I figured we'd best light a shuck out of that little canyon. I mounted up and we headed out, away from those bear. We made good time up the trail, when Old Sally started balking and snorting. I thought, More bear?"

"Was it more bear, Grandpa?"

"Nope, not more bear. Around the bend there was a grass fire that blocked the trail. The chest-high bushes, huckleberry, and the like were burning fierce. I stopped Old Sally to take stock of our situation. Behind us were three bear. Ahead of us was a raging fire. I looked to both sides of the trail. Much too steep for Sally and me to ascend. Even a mule would have struggled to get up those slopes. The fire was headed in our direction. Sally kept whinnying and backing up. I dismounted and held tight to her reins and led her back the way we came, toward the mama bear and the two yearling cubs. Sally was very unhappy about that. So was I. But the fire was more of a threat than the bear. At least I thought so.

"We slowly inched down the trail and around the bend. There stood the three bear, completely blocking the trail. Sally started rearing and snorting and making a huge fuss. She made like she was going to break away from me and charge the bear."

"What did the bear do then?"

"They stood up on their hind legs to look as threatening as they could and all three roared at Sally and me."

"Then what?"

"Sally tossed her head and rared back on her hind legs, whinnied really loud and charged the bear, dragging me along with her."

"Then what?"

"The bear ate us."

"No, they didn't."

"No. You're right. They didn't. They dropped to all fours, turned and ran down the trail away from us, as fast as they could travel. We never saw those bear again."

"Did you go try to put out that fire?"

"Nope. I followed U. S. Forest Service procedure. The aforementioned crew of Forest Service men — as fine a group of drunks and ne're-do-wells as ever I saw — arrived in horse-drawn wagons to fight the fire," Grandpa said.

"Did you help them fight the fire?"

"Not my job. I was the smoke chaser, not the fire fighter. I spotted the smoke plumes, reported, using the old hand-cranked telephone. Then I got the heck out of there."

"Did you get credit for spotting the fire?"

"Ha. Not the way it works, Davy. I actually got a reprimand from the Forest Service supervisor that went in my file."

"What for?"

"For taking too long to report the fire."

"But the bear?"

"Old Grady, the supervisor, never seen those bear. He didn't see them, so they were a figment of my imagination. An excuse for not doing a better job. He said, 'You probably stopped to eat your lunch and fell asleep in the shade, and woke up with a jolt when your horse started acting up. We don't pay your horse to spot fires. Hell, you probably fell asleep smoking one of those cigarettes of yours and started the fire yourself.'"

"That's not fair."

"Lesson learned, Davy. Life is hard. But it is not fair. Soon after that I was called to work for the NPRR. I've been there ever since. Want some more coffee with your milk? Maybe I'll fry us up a mess of eggs. How does that sound? Want yours over easy?"

"Sounds good, Grandpa."

"Okay then, Podner. You can crack 'em."

And I did. Grandpa and I ate our eggs together, and then he read me Ally Oop out of the morning newspaper funny papers.

It was just him and me at the kitchen table, early in the morning. In Thompson Falls, Montana.

FUNERAL IN WHITEPINE

My great-uncle Irvin died during World War II, when Mom and I lived with Dad's parents, Grandpa Homer and Grandma Katherine, in Thompson Falls, Montana. Uncle Irvin was Grandma Katherine's younger brother. Not the youngest boy—that was Uncle Lyle, the baby of the Haase family until Aunt Allie, my great-aunt Alice, came along years later.

Uncle Irvin's health was always bad. He had a huge goiter he refused to see a doctor about. The sight of that goiter scared me, when I was a four-year-old. He seemed to treasure it. It entered the room before him.

He was a gruff, unfriendly man in his forties. He had been married to Beulah—who died before I knew him—and they had a daughter, Carole, a tall, dark woman with a long, narrow nose. He also had a step-daughter named Doris, a small, blonde, plump woman who had a little girl named Lailah, whom I played with in the sandbox outside the boxcar that I lived in with my grandparents, my mother, and Dad's sister, Aunt Nellie Mae.

Uncle Irvin always hated and mistreated his stepdaughter Doris when she was a little girl. He'd pinch her under her ear until she sobbed. She got on his nerves. Nellie Mae said all kids and most adults got on Irvin's nerves. He blamed it on his thyroid problems, which eventually knocked him down, so he ended up in the Veterans' Hospital in Missoula, where he died.

Grandma Katherine loved her brother Irvin dearly. Of her two brothers, he was the go-getter.

His younger brother Lyle had no aspirations. He married "plain old maid" Helen, the daughter of the postmaster of Whitepine, Montana, and became postmaster himself. Plain old Helen did all the work. She'd grown up in the big old country store that was also the Post Office in Whitepine, "So it's easier for her," Uncle Lyle would say.

Lyle was so short and fat that pretty much everything was hard for him. Although Dad was not fat, Uncle Lyle was the relative that he resembled most closely physically.

Uncle Irvin had been working at Farragut Naval Training Station, just known as Farragut by most folks. To hear him tell it, he built the whole place by himself. When handbills went up all over Sandpoint, Idaho, in 1942, right after the Japs bombed Pearl Harbor, Uncle Irvin was one of the first in line to get a construction job building Farragut near Lake Pend Oreille in what had been the small town of Bayview, Idaho. Soon it was the largest city in Idaho.

Uncle Irvin made more money there than he'd made before in his life—one dollar and sixty cents an hour. As a young man, he always told us, he'd worked for "a dollar a day and found." Whatever that meant; Uncle Irvin never explained it. "And damned glad to get it," he'd add.

Grandpa Homer called him a blowhard and worse, and had always been jealous of the closeness between Katherine and Irvin.

When Grandpa was gone during the day, working his railroad job, Irvin would show up and let Katherine pamper and feed him.

This was in the twenties, well before Irvin built Farragut. Nellie Mae always said, "No love was lost between Homer and Irvin." It was rumored that their lack of love had come to a fistfight, and Homer told Irvin to "stay the hell away" when Homer was at work. Grandpa Homer would leave work early some days, come home and lurk around the homestead, peeking in the windows to catch sight of what Katherine and Irvin "were really up to."

I remember Uncle Irvin visiting Thompson Falls, just a few months before he died in Missoula from his goiter. I pictured the goiter exploding and Irvin shouting, "Damn the torpedoes, full speed ahead," one of his favorite things to say when he'd had a few too many of the long-necked beers he drank while sitting out in the sun near our boxcar home.

Uncle Irvin had none too gentle a manner with me. One time I was sitting in the doorway to the boxcar when Uncle Irvin had an urgent need to get inside quickly to use the bathroom. He hollered, "Damn the torpedoes, full speed ahead," and booted me out of the way as he hurried to the bathroom, unbuckling his overalls as he went.

Sometimes he'd sing a song about Buttonhook Bay. When he'd start singing it, Grandma Katherine always shushed him, so I suspect the song wasn't meant for young ears. Not that Irvin would care. The song started, "Swimming in Buttonhook Bay, naked as a jay..."

As Aunt Nellie Mae said, "Irvin was such an ornery guy, all us kids were scared to death of him. Even when we grew up, we steered clear of him."

When Irvin died, the reaction was mixed. Grandma was beside herself. Homer was quiet, as usual, but he seemed fine about it. Nellie Mae was like Homer. My mother had other things on her mind, probably my father's well-being as a Marine infantryman on Iwo Jima.

To me, Uncle Irvin was a big, scary guy, whom I wouldn't miss. Any man who would kick a little kid was better off dead, in my opinion.

Lyle was my favorite of the two great-uncles. When we went to Whitepine to his general store, he always had a cold Coke or an Orange Crush for me, and often an Oh Henry candy bar, too.

Helen would try to put a stop to that. "Between you and those kids, you are eating up the profits, Lyle," Helen would say from behind the counter.

"Oh, Helen, hush up. A little candy and soda pop never bankrupted anybody," Lyle would say.

She'd give Lyle one of her long-faced looks and go back to sorting the mail.

I never saw Lyle do much more than pump a tank of gas from the old glass-topped pump in front of the store. Mostly he sat on the front porch if it was a sunny day or, if not, in front of the pot-bellied woodstove inside the store, with his feet up. Life was sweet for Lyle.

And now his go-getter brother was dead.

"From overwork," Lyle said.

"That'll never happen to you," Helen said.

"Hell, no. Not if I have anything to say about it," Lyle said. "To hear him tell it, he built Farragut single-handed."

"I've never seen you pound a nail," Helen said.

"I hope you'll still be able to say that twenty years from now. I was raised for finer things."

"Like what, for instance?"

"Great thoughts."

"Share one with us," Helen said.

"I'm still polishing it."

"You are a perfectionist."

"Yes, that is my middle name, and the bane of my life," Lyle said.

I didn't believe that. I was pretty sure his middle name was Ferdinand, after his father.

Everyone wore black to the funeral of Great-Uncle Irvin, or dark blue. Except me. I had no black clothes. Mother didn't want to bring me to the funeral, but there was nobody to leave me with. So I was driven out to Whitepine, to what was basically the private Haase family cemetery.

Before we left Thompson Falls for the short drive to the tiny town of Whitepine, there was a church service in the Roman Catholic Church. I'd only ever gone to Lutheran church services, but this one seemed little different to me. There was no choir, but maybe that was a small town thing. I never asked. I was corralled between Mom and Aunt Nellie Mae. My grandmother was very quiet, no sobbing, as she wasn't the sort to sob, but she held onto Uncle Lyle, who was stuffed into a dark blue suit.

Everyone was there in the church—Uncle Bruce and Aunt Allie; Doris with Lailah, who was the only other child in attendance that I'd spent any time with. Helen, Lyle's wife, with their two children, David and Dorothy, who were years older than I, born during the 30's in the depths of the Great Depression.

I thought little of Uncle Irvin being dead and gone. I was glad I'd never see him or his goiter again.

When we stood around his open grave in the Whitepine Cemetery, and his coffin was lowered into the ground, surrounded by what seemed like the entire population of Sanders County, I thought about what a gruff and nasty man he'd been. But only briefly. Mostly, I thought of my father, the Marine on Iwo Jima, fighting Japs. I didn't want to ever be standing on wet grass, looking at a pile of dirt and a deep hole that my father would be lowered into.

If he was killed by the Japs, is that what would happen? Would they find his body on that tiny island and send it home to us like a coconut, with a shipping label attached to it with wire? I supposed they might. He'd look worse than Uncle Irvin with his ugly exploded goiter. He'd be shot.

I'd seen many deer hanging up to be dressed out, after my grandfather or uncle had shot them and brought them home. They were a bloody mess. I knew what gunshots did to an animal. A person would look even worse, with no fur on them.

I didn't shed a tear for Great-Uncle Irvin. Maybe Carole was sad. I knew they'd get over it. Uncle Irvin was no great loss to the world. I didn't believe he'd built Camp Farragut by himself. I thought that if he had not showed up there, the place would be no different at all. I was happy to know I'd never again hear him shout, "Damn the torpedoes, full speed ahead," and then have him kick me through a doorway. Great-Uncle Irvin was dead.

Nellie Mae, who was holding my hand, bent down to my ear and whispered, "We all die."

HUNTING WITH GRANDPA

Grandpa Homer and I drove far out into the hills beyond Thompson Falls, Montana, where he said he knew there was a deer waiting for us.

He'd packed our lunches, including a big thermos of hot coffee for him to drink, and a couple of bottles of Orange Crush for me, "to wash down our grub," he'd said. The sandwiches were made of thick slices of pot roast on white bread, slathered with yellow French's mustard and mayonnaise. I'd helped with the slathering.

"These ought to stick to our ribs," he'd said. "Let's go, Davy." He loaded his trusty 30.06 into the old Chevy and tossed our sack lunches into the back seat with it. "Let's go get 'em. We're loaded for bear."

"Bear?"

"No, it's just an expression. We won't see any bear. But with any luck we'll see deer, and I'll bag one of them. And you'll help me load it up." He placed his deer tag on the broad dashboard of the old car, and opened my door for me.

"How can I be of help to you, Grandpa?"

"You can be my spotter, and you can direct me. Tell me if I'm loading the deer onto the hood right." Grandpa started the car, and we rolled off into the path from the boxcars where we lived.

"Okay, I'll do my best. How will you load him up?"

"I'll have to use the laws of physics. Finesse, too. No brute force. Those days are done. This whole expedition will have to be done with finesse."

"Finesse?"

"Yes, it is a French word, meaning 'elegant use of minimal expenditure of energy.'"

"Oh. Did you learn that word in the Army?"

"Not that word. Plenty of others. I did learn the principle. There's always a hard way to do things. Also an easy way. And the Army way," he added.

"Which way will we do it?"

"We'll do it the Willson Way," he said.

"The world is hard to figure out," I said.

"You don't know the half of it, Davy."

"I don't?"

"Nope, but don't worry, you'll discover the world a little bit at a time. Today is one of those days," he said.

"Where are we going?"

"To my special sacred hunting place. I've shot a deer in this place every hunting season since we moved to Thompson Falls, and before, when we lived near Trout Creek."

"Do other people hunt there, too?"

"If they do, I've never seen them there. I think of it as my special place."

"What will I do there?"

"You can be my adviser," Grandpa said.

"But I'm only a little boy."

"But you are a keen observer. You are always watching. Always listening. The most quiet little boy I ever knew."

"I do that so there'll be no surprises. So I don't get in the way. As my Aunt Lee said, 'Little boys are a drug on the market'."

"Do you know what that means?"

"No. But it doesn't sound good to me."

"She shouldn't have said that to you." Grandpa shook his head as he pulled onto the main road.

"She didn't. She thought I was asleep. She said that to Mom."

"You won't be a drug on this market," he said. "You'll be my valued companion and my lookout. You won't let me doze off in the sunshine."

"How will we find the deer, Grandpa?"

"We won't. We'll let him find us," he said.

"Why would he want to find us? We have the gun."

"Maybe he wants to provide us with meat for our table," Grandpa said.

"That makes no sense."

"Sure it does. We need meat to live. The land supports only so many deer. They run out of food. There are too many deer now, because man has killed all the wolves. Now we have to play the part of the wolves."

I liked the idea of us being wolves.

He added, "We can't kill the deer with our teeth and claws, so I use my trusty old 30.06."

"Will you shoot the biggest deer we see?"

"No. I don't want a big, old, stringy buck. I want to shoot a young, tender buck—one that has not been knocking around the woods too long. That's the buck that's easiest to shoot. The wily old lord of the woods with the large rack of antlers is of no interest to me," Grandpa said.

We drove up and up a winding old road, deep into the hills. It was a long ride. We spotted deer several times on our way to Grandpa's favorite spot. "We don't want those deer," Grandpa told me.

Finally, he pulled his car off the road, next to a large, sloping meadow. He turned off the engine and we got out. "You carry the lunches, Davy."

I did so. The Orange Crushes were in the lunch bag. Grandpa carried the rifle and the thermos and an old Army blanket for us to sit on. We crossed the old road, and walked onto the grassland. We walked a very short distance, slowly. It was hard for Grandpa to walk far or fast. Some days he was in great pain due to arthritis, and what he called "the rhumatiz." He'd cut holes in the toes of the leather boots he was wearing, to give room for his swollen, painful toes.

We approached a large flat rock in the sun. "Let's walk around the rock carefully. Snakes really like the warmth of this rock."

We walked around the large blue rock. We spotted no rattle-snakes. "How did this big rock get here in this open meadow?" I asked Grandpa.

"I think a glacier left it here millions of years ago, so we'd have a place to sit when we hunted."

"It did?"

"Yep. Indians used to sit on this rock long ago and wait for deer to come to them to feed them for the winter. They'd make pemmican from the deer meat to tide them over the hard winters they used to have in this area. We'll make chops and roasts and hamburger out of him for our locker in town."

"Indians?"

"Yes, Indians. If you look closely at the rock surface, you'll see de-signs they etched on the rock when they waited for their deer. They used sharp pieces of chert or flint to mark the rock."

We spread our blanket out double on the bench-like side of the rock, and sat facing down the hill. Grandpa said our deer would appear down there. I looked at the smooth blue-green surface of the rock and found deerlike stick figures scratched into it. Also snakelike squiggles. I pointed them out to my grandpa.

"Yes, Davy, they thought that by scratching those figures, they were calling up the deer to come to them and feed them," Grandpa said.

"Like magic?"

"Yes, like magic. That's what we call everything we don't understand."

A large tree near the rock provided us shade. "Was that tree there when the Indians hunted here?"

"Yes. And before that. That is an ancient tree."

In an hour or so, we got hungry. Grandpa had been drinking his coffee all along. I opened an Orange Crush with the special blade on a Boy Scout knife Grandpa gave me. I drank the Orange Crush down, and enjoyed all the orange pieces that floated in the drink. Grandpa said that the coffee he drank was good for what ailed him.

"What ails you?" I asked.

"Just about everything, Davy. Getting old is a hard thing. The hardest. For a man who has worked hard all his life."

We ate our beef sandwiches. Hunting made me very hungry, with all the sitting and looking. The pot roast was really good with the mustard on it.

Grandpa said it was easier to digest the food if we were quiet. Also, our deer would arrive after we'd been quiet for about an hour. Grandpa took out his gold pocket watch and checked the time. He put a finger to his lips in a "be quiet" signal. He got his 30.06 ready. We looked down the hill to the bottom of the meadow, and we sat and said nothing for an hour. Grandpa had told me there was a creek down there we couldn't see, where deer came to drink near the end of the day when the shadows were long.

The shadows were long now.

We both saw movement down at the bottom edge of the meadow at the same time. Grandpa lifted his rifle to his shoulder. He took his shot. Boom. The shot echoed off the trees and hills.

The deer at the bottom of the gentle hill looked up, took a half-step, and fell to the ground. "That's our deer, Davy. All things come to he who waits. Patiently. Quietly."

"Now what, Grandpa?"

"We have to retrieve our young buck now, Davy."

First, we cleaned up the area around our rock. "Always leave your campsite cleaner than it was when you arrived," Grandpa told me.

I peed on our big tree, then we went and got back in our car.

Our lunch sacks were tossed in the back seat on the floor. The thermos was stowed there, too, and my empty Orange Crush bottles and Grandpa's rifle, wrapped in the Army blanket. Grandpa started up the car and carefully drove it down the gentle hill through the meadow. We could hear the grass rustling and scratching underneath us as we made our way down, until we were very close to the dead buck.

The buck had two points on each side of his rack of horns. "He's a nice young, tender one, Davy."

Grandpa used "maximum finesse" to maneuver the dead buck onto the hood of the car. "No heavy lifting, Davy," he said. "Leverage is what it is all about." He tied a rope to the buck's head, ran the rope around a small nearby tree and, by pulling on the rope and jockeying the car, got the deer up on the hood, where he tied it.

I coached and advised him as he did this.

"We'll do all the rest when we get him home," Grandpa said. "We'll call Uncle Lyle to come over to help skin and dress out the buck. He'll be happy to help us for a quarter of the meat."

And that's exactly what we did. I think Grandpa left the buck to hang from the rafters of the garage for a while. I don't remember the exact details; it was a long time ago.

I was only a little boy.

GRANDPA AND HIS MOTOR CAR

We were sitting together on Grandpa's motor car down near the shed that the cars were kept in when they were not in use. I'd wanted my picture taken with Grandpa Homer on his motor car. It seemed such a brave thing to do—to go out on the tracks on that rusty, rickety little bare-bones iron contraption to do signal and track maintenance—with all the huge trains to look out for. I thought of my grandpa as the bravest, smartest man I knew.

I asked my mom to take our picture that day, a sunny day in August. She wanted us to face into the sun so she could stand with her back to it. "That's the way to take a picture," she said.

She had rules like that for most things. That's why most of the family pictures she took are of people squinting or shielding their eyes with their hands. Grandpa and I sat on his motor car, which was off to the side of the tracks. Grandpa sat to my right, with his long legs crossed. I sat next to him, my short stubby legs hanging straight down.

We both squinted into the sun.

"Look at me," my mother said.

So I did. Right at her. Grandpa was looking off to his left, in my direction. He was dangling a cigarette that he'd rolled while Mom was gearing up to take our picture. Those were Grandpa's words: "You about geared up for this operation, Alice?"

I figured that was some old railroad expression. He had a million of 'em. Also, salty old Army expressions, and even some mining expressions. "Fire in the hole," he'd holler, when he lit a firecracker on the Fourth of July and put an old lard bucket over it.

I usually wore a hat at that age, but that day I did not. Grandpa wore his old flat cloth working-man's hat. He had iron grey hair under it—quite a lot of it. My hair looked blond in that harsh sunlight. In the distance behind us was the Thompson Falls Depot, the water tower and the boxcars that were our home during World War II.

When Mom finished taking the pictures, she said she had to walk downtown to shop for groceries for our supper. She had some meat coupons, but Grandpa told her to get some venison out of our locker—ground up into burger. She could make spaghetti and meatballs for our supper.

Mom didn't much like venison, having been raised on a diet of salmon and halibut in Ballard by a family of Norwegian Lutheran fisherfolk, but she loved Grandpa Homer and me, too, so that's what it was. "Spaghetti and meatballs for supper it'll be," Mom said.

"Good," Grandpa said.

"Good." I rubbed my tummy.

Grandpa and I were hot from sitting in the sun. Hot and thirsty. "Let's walk back home, Davy."

"Tell me a story on the way, Grandpa. Please. A story about your job."

"Okay. What kind of story?"

"One about your terrible boss, and about having to work in snow and sleet."

"That'll be easy. The hard part will be deciding which story to tell."

We walked along the railroad tracks in the sunshine, through the grass. The thrum of grasshoppers and the smell of tar and creosote hung in the air as the heat cooked them out of the railroad ties. There was nothing I loved more as a boy than to be ambling along with my grandfather. He'd rolled a new cigarette, and he smoked it as he ruminated, as he called it. "Ruminating and cogitating."

He held my hand with his free hand, which was much gnarled and bumpy. What he called "the hand of a working man." Neither of us were great walkers. He wore shoes that he'd cut out slits in the toes of, to make room for the painful bumps on his toes. What he called his "rheumatiz." Me, due to what I would come to learn were missing bones in my feet—bones I'd been born without.

Soon we got to the little Thompson Falls Park, which was some green grass and a few shade trees and a fountain. Grandpa said it was a memorial fountain for the men of Sanders County who died in World War I. It had cold, fresh water flowing out of it, "artesian water," he told me. After we drank the cold water, we settled down on a bench in the shade to "rest our barking dogs," according to Grandpa.

"Well, Davy, it seemed that it was always the middle of January when it was forty below zero that I'd get that call that the red board was up and I'd have to leave my warm bed and venture out into the black, cold night to determine if there was really a busted track, or if the red board signal was defective but the tracks were fine. No way to tell that without me going out there. To do that in the middle of the night under those conditions was an ordeal. But that was the job I'd signed up for, and it was the only job I could get. So I did my best to hang onto it. What else was I suited for? They weren't going to hire me to be the bank vice-president."

"Why not, Grandpa?"

"Men like me, from my frontier background, with Army tattoos and scarred-up hands, would scare people in a bank. I'm the sort that would be more likely to ride a horse into the bank with a shotgun to steal the money."

"Really?"

"Probably not, but I wouldn't be considered to be a bank vice-president. So I worked for the railroad, all my live long days." He half-sang those last words.

"The story, Grandpa."

"Yes, the story. It was one of those clear, cold nights, about the middle of January, and the mercury was hovering around forty below, as I mentioned earlier. I had banked the fires and let the dog in and had got nicely settled down in bed."

"What kind of dog was it, Grandpa?"

"Old Red. My Irish setter. He was a good old dog, but he hated the cold, as did I."

"Did you and old Red get to stay warm that night?"

"Old Red did. But I did not. My back was against the heater and I was cogitating about what a soft and easy life a maintainer had, when *clickety click* went the selector and *ring* went the telephone bell. Before I could jump up and answer it, *ring*, she went again, and by the time I got to the darn thing and had the receiver down it had started to *r-r-ring* again, so I just pushed the button and held the receiver up to the mouthpiece and let her *ring* in the dispatcher's ear. Just can't discourage them birds no matter how hard you try."

"Did he go deaf?"

"No such luck. Besides, he still had his other ear," Grandpa said.

"Then what?"

"The dispatcher had to determine it was me, which it was. Who else would be stupid enough to be there in the middle of the night awaiting his call, which usually never comes? Then he told me that number so-and-so reports a red board down at your last signal on the west end; better go down there and find out what's the matter."

"So did you go?"

"Well, I try to dissuade the dispatcher. I says, 'Mr. Dispatcher, it's forty below. I just went out and looked; besides, the rail is slippery as all get-out from ice.' The dispatcher didn't care. He said, 'I know,

I know, but there might be a broken rail, and it is only fifteen miles down there, so git a wiggle on and scram.'"

"So what did you do then? Did you get a wiggle on and scram?"

"Well, I put on all the rags I could find around the shack, and got a wiggle on and scrammed. I headed for the motor car garage, which in no wise was steam heated. After torching up old Direct Drive Adams and sanding down the rail for about ten rail lengths, I finally got her a goin'. And hopped on the saddle. Suffice it to say that hind wheel travelled about two hundred miles trying to make the fifteen miles between the car garage and the red board."

"What did you find when you got to the red board, Grandpa?"

"Well, miracle of miracles, when I arrived there, the red board was red. I lost no time getting the torch lit so I could thaw out the lock. No, the heat didn't make her go clear; it was a top post mechanism."

"What's that Grandpa?"

"It'd take too much time to explain it and that would slow the story down to a dead stop, Davy."

"Okay, Grandpa."

"Finally the door was open, and I found the track relay de-energized, which indicated track trouble. This track section was only one and seven-tenths miles long, so I fought Old Adams on the slippery rail until I got her going, and away toward the bizness end of that track section we went."

"Was it really cold out there, Grandpa?"

"Yes, Davy, it was cold. Did I mention it was forty degrees below zero? Don't ever get a job working outside in Montana in the winter. Don't."

"I won't, Grandpa."

"I had to stop several times to put the meter on the track, to see if I had passed by the open or not. After about the second stop, I couldn't get Old Liz started anymore—guess she just got tired of so much stopping and starting—so I threw her off the track, and started on foot, testin' every hundred yards or so. And I finally found it, a broken rail, just three lengths from the energy end of that long track section. I had walked at least one-and-one-fourth miles through the hard snow and forty below, because I couldn't tell while riding along on the motor car where my track juice was cut off. "

"You must have been shivering, Grandpa."

"By that time, I was too cold to shiver, Davy. About the time I got back to Old Liz, which was about two hours after I had started on the testing jamboree, I had a bright idea hit me, *bang!*"

"What was that idea, Grandpa?"

"Sit tight and I'll tell you all about it, Davy."

I did sit tight and he did tell me about it. All I remember about it was that he invented a device that made a flashlight connection with the rails, so when the rail was broken, the connection would break too, and the light would blink to show that there was a problem. Which saved the stopping and starting on slipper rails. I still have his patent application papers for that device.

He said that he thought that the invention might make him rich, but it did not. "Some East Coast shyster applied a week earlier than I did."

"Did he get rich?"

"I suspect he did." Grandpa got out his railroad watch from the small pocket of his work pants and consulted it. He showed it to me. It had his name, Homer Willson, signed on it in gold. "Tempus fugit, Davy. We'd better get back home and cleaned up for our supper. Your mom will be getting our spaghetti and meatballs on the table in no time at all. I don't want her to toss it out if we're not there, Johnny on the spot, with our sleeves rolled up and our forks at attention."

"Mom wouldn't throw supper out, Grandpa."

"Your mom wouldn't. Your grandma Katherine might," he said.

"Do you have other stories to tell me about the life of a railroad man?"

"I do. Next time I'll tell you the story of the time my motor car got run over by the First, Number 2, near Mile Post 41, and demolished. The miserable bastard, my supervisor, Mr. T. E. Housley, cited and suspended me. I explained to him my watch was slow, but he did not care."

I patted Grandpa's arm.

We stepped up to our boxcar home and took off our shoes before going inside to the kitchen. Grandpa lit up another cigarette. "It's a hard life, Davy, but a plate of hot chow helps mitigate that. And a cigarette."

"Yes, Grandpa," I said.

GRANDPA AND THE SLOW WATCH

"It's a tale of moral turpitude and duplicity," Grandpa said.

I had no idea what he was talking about, but his voice was sad.

"An old man always wants to set a good example for his grandson. That's not always possible. All of us have shortcomings," he said.

That couldn't be possible. My grandpa didn't have shortcomings.

"The life of a working man is a hard one. Hard work beats a man down. Demoralizes him. Pushes him into a corner. When a man is cornered, he becomes like a rat. He just wants to get out alive. To live another day.

"It could easily have been me that day that got pulverized by that train—the First, Number 2—near Mile Post 41. But I left the motor car on the track—directly contravening all rules, which were clear to me. 'The signal maintainer must remove the motor car from the tracks while checking, trouble-shooting or performing routine maintenance on a defective signal.' I figured I had enough time. I figured wrong."

"Why didn't you move the motor car off the tracks, Grandpa?"

"I used to be able to do it easily. Finesse and leverage could do it. The older I got, the more broken down I got, the more crippled I became from arthritis, the less finesse I had, the less leverage I could access. And I had no more brute strength at all. Years ago, I could just bull that damned thing on and off the tracks. But officially, it weighs nine hundred pounds. I tried to strip off every extraneous part to make it lighter, but even then, it still weighs eight hundred pounds, and it feels like a ton."

I could see the strain and pain on my grandpa's face. I reached out and patted his arm.

"So I left it on the track. That signal was not an 'on again, off again, Finnegan' affair. It was seriously messed up. It appeared the wires had been chewed on by a rat. I had to strip the insulation off the wires, replace some of them, tape the whole thing up, and seal it from moisture and condensation, and that took time. I lost track of time. I was totally focused on the job in front of my nose. I didn't hurry it. I did it right. I forgot all about the scheduled First, Number 2, train. Until I heard it coming. And then it was too late.

"I hardly had time to duck around behind the signal post for protection from flying debris, let alone time to yank that motor car off the tracks. The train came around the bend, braked with a screech, but proceeded to run over that motor car and smash it into a million oily pieces. It was a miracle the shrapnel didn't hit me. One sharp piece of the car hit the post I was behind, and stuck in it like a stiletto. If it had pierced me, that would have been the end of me. I would have been dead where I stood. I wouldn't be here today to regale you with this tale.

"There was fear on the part of the engineer that I was aboard that motor car. They were relieved I was okay. They cleaned the debris off the tracks, and gave me a ride to Thompson Falls, and then the brouhaha really started."

"The what started, Grandpa?"

"The brouhaha. The unholy fuss. The enquiry. It was as though Torquemada himself had taken charge. The accusations and recriminations and blame. All of those flew thicker and faster than the pieces of that shattered motor car. The signal supervisor, T. E. Hausley, wanted to fire me. Well, he really wanted my head on a pike. He never was a friend of mine. He hated me."

"Why would he hate you, Grandpa?"

"Because I was a union man to the core. I never crossed a picket line during a strike. His favorite worker was my kiss-ass brother-in-law, A. R. Johnson. A. R. never honored anything. He was a money grubber. All for himself. The greater good meant nothing to A. R. He crossed picket lines and built up seniority over me, so he could bump me from any job or station I put in for. He did it time and time again. He took joy in doing it. No seniority was built up during strikes. And a strike could go on for months. So that bastard always lorded it over me—that scab, scissorsbill SOB."

Grandpa was silent for a long time. He took out a sack of Bull Durham and some papers and rolled himself a cigarette. He reached over to the kitchen range and scratched a wooden kitchen match and lit the cigarette. He took a long drag on it. "Where were we?"

"A. R. was a scab and a scissorsbill SOB," I said.

"You are a good listener, Davy," Grandpa said.

"Thanks, Grandpa."

"Let me get the letter I got sent by the signal supervisor, T. E. Hausley." Grandpa went over to the big old trunk and rummaged for a few minutes until he came up with the letter.

He read the date to me first. "July 13, 1943: Tacoma, Washington."

"I thought it happened longer ago than that, Grandpa," I said.

"Nope, it's recent history, Davy. But in terms of your short life, it was a long time ago, over half your life ago. For me, it's just an eyeblink ago. You were just learning to walk." Grandpa reached into the pocket of his work shirt and pulled out his beat-up old diary. He opened it up and pointed to some pages. "See, Davy?"

I could see it but, of course, I couldn't read it. I thought I could read my book, *Poky Little Puppy*, but I really couldn't. I had it memorized, so when Mom skipped a page, I knew. But I couldn't read it, and I couldn't read the tiny, scrawled writing of my grandpa's diary. "Read it to me, please, Grandpa," I said.

"Right here." He pointed to the bottom of the page. "'7-13, 14, 15, oiled east end and fixed bond wires. Davy walked the 14th,'" he read.

"You wrote it in your diary."

"Yes, I did. I liked to keep track of momentous events, and also the picayune ones." He thumbed back a couple of pages and read to me, "'Worked on corroded signal wires. Motor car hit by 1st/#2 at 11:27 A. M. My watch 25 minutes slow.'"

"Was your watch slow, Grandpa?"

"No. No, it was not. That's where the duplicity entered this scenario. Before the gang of railroaders converged on me, I opened up my watch, unscrewed the back, and set it back twenty-five minutes. That watch never lost one minute of time in a month. It never did. I felt terrible, blaming my plight on the innocent watch. Nobody bought it anyhow."

"But you didn't get fired," I said.

"Nope. Their hands were tied."

"Really?"

"No. It's an expression. I meant the war. The war has taken away all the young men. Left the railroad manned by a bunch of stove-in old geezers and gummers. But we're the best they can do now, and until the war ends. I figure, when the war ends, all the chickens will come home to roost and my time working for the Northern Pacific Railroad will end."

Grandpa picked up the letter he'd dug out of the trunk and began to read it to me:

"'Mr. Homer Willson:

"'On May 31st you had your motor car struck and demolished by 1st/2 near Mile Post 41, and from the investigation of this accident it is very clear to me that had you observed the rules and removed the motor car from the track while working, the accident would not have happened regardless of the fact your watch was slow.

"'You should understand that rule violation is a matter that cannot be tolerated and were it not for the fact that we are at this time very short on help you would be given an actual suspension of possibly 3o days duration for your negligence. However, this is to advise you that you have been given a 1o day record suspension with the proviso that if within a reasonable time there should be another rule violation on your part, you will not only be given the actual suspension that may be warranted from such violation, but in addition you will serve an actual 1o days for your motor car accident.

"'I wish again to emphasize the fact that there is absolutely no excuse for having a motor car struck by regular trains on time.

"'Signed: T. E. Housley.'" He slammed the letter down on the kitchen table, causing coffee to spill out of his mug.

"What does that all mean, Grandpa?"

"Well you might ask, Davy. It would be too much to expect that a signal supervisor could communicate in plain English, let alone demonstrate a particle of compassion for a broke-down old railroad man who's slaved away the best years of his life for the NPRR.

"That fat, mealy-mouthed bastard, T. E. Housley, has not lifted anything heavier than a coffee mug in the past twenty years, if ever. 'No excuse,' he says, for having a motor car struck. He knows I had a double hernia operation in Missoula at the railroad hospital one month prior to the accident. He knows that. It is a matter of record.

"When I brought it up at the hearing, all he had to say about that was that the railroad doctor had signed me off as 'One-hundred-percent fit to return to full-time duty.' Would a railroad doctor lie? Would he? He sure as hell would. He knew what side of his bread the butter was on. It would be his job on the line if he did not. As it was, they wanted me back at work two weeks earlier. Housley pressured him about that. It's just like the Army, Davy. All we are is cannon fodder. Housley would have fired me if he could, but there's nobody to take my place."

"Could Housley fix a signal?"

"He could as easily fly to the moon on gossamer wings as fix a signal, Davy. Not many of us can keep patching up those old signals to make 'em work. Can't get the parts we need due to the war effort. But the NPRR is part of the war effort. Moving troops and war materiel. So old Housley had to swallow his pride, write nasty things about me for my file, but keep me doing my job. But his letter did the trick. I could feel the black dogs chewing at me in the night. Nightmares that chilled my blood. All I ever wanted was a job where I'd be appreciated, Davy."

"Did you ever have one, Grandpa?"

"Yes, one. When I was in the Army at Fort Missoula. I made corporal. But then they took it away from me. On a technicality. The U. S. Army said there were too many corporals. My captain called me in and apologized to me when he took away my stripe. He hated to do it, but he was ordered to do it. I never had that much power and responsibility again. It's a mean old world, Davy. A mean old world." He got up from the table and made his way over to the trunk, walking as if he had broken glass in his shoes. He put the letter back in the trunk. Slammed the lid.

"I've told you before. Don't be a working man, Davy. Go to college. You are a bright boy. A smart boy. In college, you'll learn wonderful things. Read the classics. Learn a foreign language. That's the ticket to a sweet life, Davy. Don't forget."

"I won't forget, Grandpa."

"Promise."

"I promise."

PILLAR, FIVE: BALLARD ONCE AGAIN

THE WAR ENDS

Grandpa listened to his radio every morning before he went to work. He'd sit at the kitchen table and drink his coffee, smoke a Camel, and listen to the radio, turned down low. Thompson Falls, Montana, was down in the bottom of a deep valley, so radio reception was "iffy," as Aunt Nellie Mae would put it. But that day, when I came into the kitchen, the radio reception was good.

Grandpa looked up at me. "The Japs are beat," he said. "Your dad will be coming home."

I climbed up onto the chair next to his. "What happened?"

"We dropped a big bomb. Two big bombs. A-Bombs. The Japs have had it," Grandpa said.

"Did lots of soldiers die?"

"No, we dropped the bombs on their cities. Real people died."

"I'm glad that didn't happen to us," I said.

"Well, nobody will ever drop a bomb on Thompson Falls."

"Why?"

"We're not important enough," he said. "Not important at all."

I thought to myself, There's a good reason to not ever be important. Keep your head down. Don't call attention. "Dad will be home soon?"

"Not soon. The Army moves slow. And the Navy moves slower. But your dad will come home," Grandpa said. "It won't be easy. Millions of veterans coming home at the same time. Like when my dad came home from the Civil War. People starved. Veterans couldn't get jobs. Tough times. All times are tough for the working man."

I didn't know then what he was talking about.

"Time for me to go to work," he said. He got up from the kitchen table. I could hear his knee joints crack. He moved slow. He put his coffee cup in the sink. Got his black lunchbox off the counter, and his thermos of coffee. Put on his rough red-and-black wool coat, and his cap. "Don't ever be a working stiff, Davy. Go to college. Get as many degrees as you can. Don't ever work for the railroad. Don't ever start smoking either."

"Which is worse?"

Grandpa laughed. "Working is worse. Smoking is a close second." He opened the door, and was gone.

Grandma was already at work, sitting in front of the telephone switchboard downtown. Mom was still asleep. She hated early mornings. So I was on my own for a while. I got the newspaper out of the woodbox next to the trash-burning stove, and tried to read it. I could make out some short words on the front page. I could stumble through the comics page, figuring out what was going on from the pictures.

I was eager to read. But that was two years away, my mom said. Even then, I hated waiting. I wanted what I wanted now. I wanted to read. I wanted my dad back home from the war. I was still afraid something bad would happen to him. His boat could sink. He could get a fever. All kinds of bad things lurked. I had a gift for thinking of the bad things that could happen.

Mom would sing to me, "Look on the sunny side, Look on the sunny side. The sunny side of life." I had trouble seeing the sunny side. I was surrounded by the gloomy side. All around me and on all sides. I couldn't even glimpse the sunny side.

When we heard from Dad, he told us when he'd get back, and he said he wanted us to wait for him in Seattle at Grandma Alma's. He would be "demobbed" in Seattle.

"What's that mean?" I asked.

Mom didn't know, but it had to happen before he came back to us.

Mom was very unhappy that Dad insisted we go back to Seattle to meet him there. She wanted to stay in Montana with Dad's parents. "But the problem is, your dad doesn't get along with his mother any better than I get along with mine," she said.

"Why?"

"Well, your dad doesn't like his mom's cooking. He thinks she'll poison him with mushrooms she gleans from the roadside."

"Would she?"

"Probably not. But she loves to get food your father says is 'suspicious.' Like rabbits from the Friels, who raise them for food. Your father hates that. He loves the food Grandma Alma cooks and serves."

"I do, too. But I like Grandma Katherine's food, too. Especially the huckleberry pie," I said.

"Your father likes the huckleberry pie, too. His problem is with the dinners she serves."

So a couple of weeks later, we took the train back to Seattle. We rode the bus to Ballard, carrying our little striped suitcase. The bus let us off near 5oth, near Grandma's big house on the corner, after we'd transferred a couple of times. The bus station had been a "madhouse," according to Mom. "Absolute bedlam," she said.

There were sailors, soldiers, Marines everywhere, meeting their loved ones. Kissing, hugging, crying. Some were fighting. I saw a woman, carrying a little baby, get knocked to the floor by a sailor. The police put handcuffs on the sailor and dragged him away. He was screaming something about the baby.

I asked my mother, "What was that all about?"

"The sailor wasn't happy to see his wife with a new baby."

"Will my dad be happy to see me?"

"As happy as he gets," Mom said. "You were here when he left. Men hate surprises. Your dad is no different."

At Grandma Alma's, our welcome was quiet. "The prodigals return," she said.

"What's a prodigal?" I asked my mom later.

"People who went away and then returned," she said.

"Grandma didn't seem happy to see us."

"We left under a cloud. Remember?"

"Oh, Grandpa Hulver's wine."

"Yes, the wine. Grandma Alma will not let that go. She's got a long memory when people try to deceive her, and she doesn't want Grandpa to have any fun or any secrets. Or any of the rest of us, either."

"Well, she said she'd made me cinnamon rolls, and would have a plate of them for me in the kitchen when I wanted them," I said. "With lots of butter on them, the way I like them."

"Yes, I heard that." She added, in a low voice, "For some reason, she has a soft spot for you in her hard heart. There's no rhyme or reason to it."

"No?"

"No," Mom said.

In Ballard, we lived in Grandma Alma's basement again. I'd play on the sidewalk out front. There was a fire hydrant there, and I'd pretend it was my dad, returned from the war.

I'd practice what I would say to my daddy when he came back from being a Marine. I only half believed he'd come back. It seemed a lot easier to believe the Japs would kill him, than that he'd get away from them. I wondered, why not just leave behind all those Japs on Iwo, in the holes they dug? Go somewhere else. Go around them. I asked my Uncle Lud that question.

He said, "We can't do that. We have to root them all out. Every last one of them. One at a time, if that's what it takes."

"They'll run out of food and die if we just leave them alone there."

"You're just a little boy. You don't understand war," he said.

Lud was right. I didn't at all. "Do you wish you were there with Dad, killing Japs?"

"I'm doing my part at Boeing. A big part of the war effort," he said. "We can't all be carrying guns."

"Dad wasn't doing his part at Boeing as an expediter?"

Uncle Lud was very quiet for the longest time. "Well," he finally answered, "I guess the government thought he'd be a better Marine than an expediter."

"Did they come and watch him work to see what he did at Boeing?"

"I don't think they had time to do that."

"So, they could have grabbed you, too," I said.

"No, they wouldn't want me." He tapped his glasses. "I can't see without them. Your dad's got perfect eyesight."

"So, no Marines wear glasses?"

"No. No, they don't. What if the glasses got broken? They'd stumble into things. It wouldn't be safe. My country is better off with me at Boeing."

"All my other uncles got grabbed up. Uncle Roy and Uncle Bob."

"Yes, they did. But Roy got a fever. And your Uncle Bob is working on the railroad, doing a job like he did in Montana, but just in India."

"So, he's safe there?" I asked.

"Maybe not. I don't know. But he's not a Marine on Iwo Jima."

"No, he isn't. I guess that is the worst," I said.

"Probably is."

My mother walked into the room. "What are you two talking about?"

"Nothing," Uncle Lud and I both said at the same time. And that was the end of that conversation.

So now, after all the fretting and worrying, my dad would come home to us, I told myself. Things would be normal again.

FATHER'S HOMECOMING

So there we were, Mom and I, in Ballard, living in the basement of Grandma's boarding house on the corner of West 50th. We waited and prepared for Fathers' return from Guam and Iwo Jima. This is where he'd made it clear that he wanted us to be. Even though Mother had wanted to stay in Thompson Falls, Montana, with Dad's parents, living by the Northern Pacific railroad tracks near the depot and just across the street from what there was of the downtown business district—the grocery store, the Post Office, the telephone office with the switchboard, the hardware store, the gas station, and a few bars and taverns.

Ballard, a small part of Seattle, was ten times bigger than all of Thompson Falls. When I was a little boy, I didn't realize Ballard was part of Seattle. I thought it was a city of its own—a very strange city.

My mom told me this story about when she was a new mother of twenty, toting me around Ballard, showing off her new baby. She would be stopped on the street, as she walked the few blocks from her house to her mother's house, by nosy old crones. "Vere you get dat baby? Dat not your baby."

Mother was blonde, tiny, blue-eyed, very fair, and she was carrying me—a dark baby. I was dark-eyed, dark haired, and very fat, with a big head and slanted eyes. I looked at least half Chinese, I've been told, and my infant photographs bear this out.

Mother says she cried at my birth when the doctor showed me to her. She told him, "That's not my baby."

"Yes, it is your baby," the doctor said.

"But he's dark."

"Yes, he is," the doctor said.

She told me she expected a blond, blue-eyed baby. That's how babies looked in Ballard. All of them. All but me. Did I have a dark father? Not really. My father did have dark hair, but light eyes and very fair skin. So, "Vere you get dat baby?" I'm blamed for having a dark great-grandmother on my father's side, Great-Grandmother Haase. She had brown eyes, the only brown eyes in the family woodpile that anyone recalled.

It was easier for mother when she got out of Ballard. In Thompson Falls, there were many brown-eyed people with dark skin. They called them Indians. And when we were in California, such folks were common, too. They called them Mexicans there.

Later, when my parents' siblings had their children after the war, their kids were all blue-eyed and fair, even the kids they adopted. But when my sister was born she, too, had brown hair and brown eyes, like me. So it goes.

Anyway: Mother did not want to be back in Ballard living in her mother's house in the basement, but Father insisted, so we took the train from Thompson Falls to Seattle and rode the bus to Ballard, carrying our little striped suitcase.

I went back to playing with my little cars and trucks in the dirt outside the kitchen door. Also, for a change of pace, I would walk around the big house on the sidewalk, and pretend the fireplug on the corner near the house was my father, returned from the war.

I'd practice what I would say to him by talking to the fireplug. I'd have to answer for the fireplug Father, as if it were like the Tar Baby, and had nothing to say for itself. I'd say, "I've been a good boy while you were gone, Daddy, just as you told me to do in your letters."

"I knew you would be, Davy," I'd have the fireplug Father say.

My father wrote letters to my mother during the months he was gone to be a Marine, and in each letter he'd enclose a short letter for me. "Dear Davy, Be a good boy and take care of your mommy," that sort of thing.

I wish I had those letters to read and refer to now, but they are long gone. Years ago, when I asked my mother for them, she told me, "Oh, we burned those in 1985, when your father was dying of brain cancer."

The notes to "Dear Davy" didn't amount to much, but they were proof to me that my father loved me and thought about me while he was away being a Marine. I pretended the fireplug was my returned father, and he was glad to see me, Davy.

One day I was at the corner with the fire hydrant when my Uncle Ludwig came home from his shift at Boeing. "What are you up to out here on the corner, Davy?"

I told him.

"We need to have a chat, Davy," Uncle Lud said.

"Okay. What about?"

"Let's go into Grandma's kitchen. I think Ma might have some cinnamon rolls there for us. And a glass of cold milk for you," he said.

So that is what we did. We went into the kitchen, which smelled of Grandma's cinnamon rolls, the best smell in the world to me up to that point in my life. We sat at the old oak kitchen table with the red-and-white-checkered oilcloth tablecloth.

We ate rolls and drank milk. Well, I drank milk; Uncle Lud drank a cup of coffee, which Grandma had on the back burner all day long. It was a Norwegian-American household, after all. Uncle Lud had a huge warm cinnamon roll on a plate with fresh butter on it, and Grandma buttered mine and cut it into four pieces. Lud ate his roll with a fork. I used my fingers.

Grandma left to deal with the wash she had going in the basement. Running a boarding house kept her busy all day long, "From dawn until the midnight sun," as she put it.

"I'm working with a couple of veterans in my department at Boeing, Davy," Uncle Lud said.

"Veterans?"

"Yes, men who are recently returned from the war."

"Killing Japs, like my dad?"

"Well, no, they were in Europe, fighting the Germans, but they had a hard war," he said.

"Did my dad have a hard war?"

"Yes, I am afraid he did." Uncle Lud dug into his roll. "These veterans I work with don't do well with noise. I dropped a hammer on the concrete floor and one of them jumped a mile, and the other one, he dropped to the floor. I guess they thought it was a gunshot." He stopped and looked at me.

I looked back at him.

"I guess my point is that your dad might come home changed. He's due here tomorrow. He could arrive a little bit jumpy."

"Jumpy?"

"Yes. You are a noisy little boy. When you come into a room, you startle me, and make me jump, and I spent the war working at Boeing. Your father spent the war fighting the Japanese."

"So, I must be very quiet? Creep around?"

"Well, yes, something like that," Uncle Ludwig said.

"I had to do that in California with Mom and Aunt Lee. Nobody there wanted a little boy around. Aunt Lee said, 'You are as welcome as the pox.'"

"The pox?"

"That's what she said."

"That's harsh," Uncle Ludwig said. "Of course, your Aunt Lee was sick a lot as a kid, and liked the house to be very quiet."

"Aunt Lee said that when she has her little boy, he'll be a quiet little boy, well-behaved—a model citizen, not a rowdy like me."

"Well, we'll see, won't we? Meanwhile, let's eat our cinnamon rolls before they get cold."

So that's what we did. Grandma's cinnamon rolls were the best.

Dad got home the next day. He was wearing his Marine Corps uniform and carrying what he called a seabag. It was heavy and it hit the floor with a thunk. I tried to be very quiet, but it was hard for me. I was very happy to have my daddy back from the war. I looked him over carefully. He looked okay to me, but maybe his eyes were a little different. Time would tell. He hugged me and Mom, and said he was happy to be home.

The next many days were a whirlwind. Things weren't the way I'd imagined them to be when I pretended the fire hydrant was my returned father. He never had time to pull me in my little Bull Dog wagon, or to toss me a ball, or to teach me how to swim. Dad would get annoyed with me if I even asked him to play with me. "Play comes after work, and work is never done," he'd say. I heard that from him a million times before I quit asking him.

We never even had a talk about what he did while he was gone.

Things weren't anything like I'd hoped they would be after the Japs were all killed. I'd still pretend the fire hydrant was my returned father. I was grateful my real father was back, but I wished he was the way I remembered him. Before he left for the Marines, he was patient with me, even when I was colicky. He'd take me on the top of his belly on the sofa, turn on the radio, and hold me tight to him and sing along with Bing Crosby. I'd forget about my stomachache and fall asleep.

Of course, I had no colic now, and Father couldn't stand having the radio on, not even Bing Crosby. As Uncle Ludwig had warned me, Father was jumpy about everything.

He was also very changeable. I guess he'd demanded that Mom and I move back to Seattle from Thompson Falls because he'd planned to attend the University of Washington, to finish the degree that he'd started at the Montana School of Mines in Butte back in the 3o's. But the registrar at the University of Washington was not impressed with Dad's School of Mines credits. He wanted Father to "start over from scratch."

That news put my father in a blind rage—a state we'd see him in often.

He wrote the registrar at the University of Montana. They offered him a good deal, back in "God's Country," as Father called it. "Those big city folks always want to screw over a country boy," he ranted.

Mom tried to calm him down. I just stayed out of his way.

We did not stay in Seattle long. We left for Thompson Falls and, soon after, moved to Missoula, where Father completed his college education. During that time and after, Father had no time for the family. He went to school, worked part-time as a typist for the registrar office, and spent a lot of time hunting to put meat on the table. My mother was busy with her new baby, my sister Leanne. This was the family pattern for the next fifteen years. Then I graduated from high school and went off to college.

The fire hydrant Father never appeared. I have a black and white photo of me by that fire hydrant, with a wistful look on my round face. My mother took the photo, but I'm sure she had no idea what was on my mind.

We didn't talk about such things.

POST, SIX: AFTER THE WAR

CODA: COWRIE SHELLS

When my father returned home from World War II, he brought with him a handful of shells he called cowrie. They were small, shiny, greenish and white, and unlike any shells I'd found on the beach at Golden Gardens in Ballard.

He said they could be found on the beaches of Iwo Jima and Guam, the islands in the Pacific he'd recently left behind. I loved these small glass-like shells. I loved how they rattled and clicked when I held them in my hand and rolled them around and admired them.

When I showed them to my grandpa Homer, he knew what they were by name. He said he'd encountered them when he'd served in the Army in 1910 in the Philippines. He said that many people used them as money. He also said that they could be used in a game like dice. He showed me how to throw a few of them onto the top of the coffee table—how some of them would land curved-side-up, and others with the white toothy side up.

"Bets were made on how many would land which-a-way," he said. Grandpa and I would play that game sometimes for fun.

Now, sixty-eight years later, I wonder where that handful of shiny, clicking cowrie shells have gone. I've dug through various boxes looking for them. So far, I've found one cowrie shell. It was in the bottom corner of an old Army ammo box I've used for boyhood keepsakes since the early 1950's.

One shell only.

I vaguely remember placing some in a goldfish bowl to decorate the white sand on the bottom. Did they get tossed out? Or are they in a sack or a box on a shelf in the garage, lost under the weight of other stuff that's misplaced or unaccounted for in my life? That's a long list of stuff. I've a good memory for those lost things. They eat away at me: a throwing knife, hand-made from the steel of a crosscut saw; a geologist's pick; an old telescope like you see pirates use in movies.

I don't remember what happened to the throwing knife or the old telescope. One day I looked for them. and they were nowhere to be found.

I remember exactly what happened to the geologist's pick. It had been forged for my father, and was his father's gift to him when he left home to become a freshman at the Montana School of Mines. It was a thing of great beauty and utility. I ill-advisedly loaned it to a young woman who worked as a welfare caseworker in the same office I worked in when I was just back from Vietnam. She left it behind at the geologic site she'd visited.

She was nonchalant about it. No real apology. "It's gone. Get over it."

It was the late 60's. Personal responsibility was in short supply. She didn't get why I was upset. "If you didn't want it to get lost, you shouldn't have lent it to me," she said, with a toss of her blonde head and a heave of her unfettered bosom.

Good point. Lesson learned. The hard way. The only way I ever learned any lesson.

What lesson did I learn from the missing handful of cowrie? I'd really like to have all of them now. I'd sit at the kitchen table with them in my hand, click them in my palm, and then toss them on the hardwood surface of the table. See how many landed-teeth-side-up and how many didn't. Remember doing that with Grandpa Homer at the kitchen table in the college housing we lived in on Flathead Street in Missoula, on the University of Montana campus, right on the golf course.

The golf course, part of it, had been gobbled up as pre-fab housing was built for returning veterans and their families, which was my father, my mother, me and my sister, and sometimes my grandfather Homer. Our housing unit was tiny: living room, kitchen, bathroom, two tiny bedrooms.

No real room for Grandpa Homer, but he often came and stayed with us for weeks at a time. He slept on the couch. He was getting medical care at either the VA Hospital or the railroad hospital, depending on whether his medical problems were caused by his time in the Army in the Philippines, or his twenty-five years as a signal maintainer for the Northern Pacific Railroad. Or his time in Libby, Montana, mining vermiculite. Or his time in the copper mines in Anaconda, when he first got back from the Army.

"Everything you ever worked at was guaranteed to cripple you, Pop," my father said, many times, in that blaming tone he had a patent on.

"What would you have me to do, work as a bank vice president?" Grandpa Homer would respond in his always soft, resonate voice.

"That makes no sense. You know I don't mean that. And could you wait until I leave for work to start clicking those damned seashells?"

"Cowrie," I said.

"What?" Father asked.

"Cowrie," I said. "People used to use them for money."

"I found them on the beach," Father said.

"I know. You told me."

"That sound they make is damned annoying. A man can't hear himself think. I've got important stuff to think about," he said.

"And Davy and I don't," Grandpa said.

"No, you don't. You are an old man. Davy is a kid. And together you make more noise than a brass band playing a Souza march."

"Bob," Mom said.

"You, too? What?"

"You're going to wake up the baby."

At that moment, Leanne let out a howl. She was in the bedroom napping. She and I shared the small, thin-walled room. Her crib was in one corner. My bunk bed was in the opposite corner, right by the window. I slept in the top bunk. Wiggletail, my Cocker spaniel, slept on the floor on a little rug that was his own. He was in the kitchen now with Grandpa and me. He didn't like all the loud voices. Especially Dad's angry voice scared him. It scared me, too.

I don't think it scared Grandpa Homer. I don't think much scared him. After all, he'd served in the Army in the Philippines, and Moros would sneak into his barracks at night and cut the throats of sleeping soldiers with their bolos. Soldiers who thought they were safe in their bunks.

Mom had been eavesdropping when Grandpa had told me that story, and she'd landed on him like a ton of bricks. "That's not a story for a little boy," she'd said. "Don't you have a brain in your old head?"

"Alice, he'll soon enough get drafted and he'll be wearing an Army uniform in some hot little no-name country with the natives after him."

"That's not going to happen," Mom had said.

Grandpa had also showed me a shoebox of old postcards from his time in the Army. They'd showed him and his buddies in uniform, and also ditches full of dead Moros. Mom didn't know about that.

* * *

Mom now had Leanne on her hip, trying to get her to stop crying. Good luck.

"This place is like a boiler factory," Father said. He got his school stuff together. The neighbors were pounding on our walls, telling us to be quiet. "I'll be back for dinner. What are you serving?"

"Venison stew," Mom said. "And baking powder biscuits."

Father left without another word. Grandpa and I went back to our game with the cowrie.

"Dad didn't know that cowrie could be used to play a game," I said to Grandpa.

"Bob isn't a game player. He never liked games. He sees them as a waste of time. He thinks that my interest in cribbage and other games of chance has kept me from getting ahead in life," Grandpa said.

"Has it?"

"Nope. I have no education. Get an education, Davy. Otherwise, you'll spend your life doing low-level work, like using a pick and shovel or a hammer and a saw, with a knucklehead boss who lords it over you at the slightest excuse. And you'll end up a stove-in old cowpoke like me."

"You said you never worked as a cowboy."

"Not exactly. But close enough. I've had a rib broke by being kicked by a cow."

"How did that happen?"

"I was assisting a cow to give birth, and I stood in the wrong spot. That's all it took," he said.

"I'll try not to get involved with cows."

"That's a start. Always study hard in school. Your dad was always a hard studier in school. He had to be. Nothing came easy for him in school, but he always would stay up late, studying. So he got into the Montana School of Mines in Butte. It was a struggle for him.

He dropped out, went to Seattle to work at Boeing to earn that big wartime money."

"Now he's back in school."

"Yes, he is. He has learned his lesson. I'm sure he'll finish this time," Grandpa Homer said. "Let's finish up this game, so I can take a nap."

So we did finish it up. I won the next roll.

I never played the cowrie game with Father. He was busy applying himself in school. He did finish up this time, and then he got a good job teaching high school in Drummond, Montana, where he'd graduated a few years earlier. We lived in more pre-fab government housing there, and I had an open sewer to play in, where I tied a long string to a dead rat's tail and pretended it was a speedboat.

But that is another story.

ABOUT THE AUTHOR

David Allen Willson was born in Seattle, Washington, on June 30, 1942, on what his mother remembered as the hottest day of the summer. During WWII, while his father served as a Marine on Iwo Jima, he lived with his mother in a series of tourist cabins in California, in his maternal grandmother's Seattle basement, and in a boxcar in Montana.

He learned to write in first grade in Missoula, Montana, and realized then that he wanted to grow up to write books—probably about war, as there was so much of it to write about. As fate would have it, he had the chance to experience war first-hand—appropriately, behind a typewriter: he was drafted into the U. S. Army in the '6os and sent to Viet Nam. He was the best soldier he knew how to be, and he received the Army Commendation Medal for his service in the Inspector General's Office.

For war writing, he has published three semi-autobiographical novels: *REMF Diary*, *The REMF Returns*, and *In the Army Now*. And now, this volume.

David has been the editor of *Viet Nam War Generation Journal*, and a contributor to *Vietnam War Literature: An Annotated Bibliography*. He has been a regular reviewer of war literature for both print and on-line editions of the VVA (Vietnam Veterans of America) *Veteran*, and has authored many other articles for the magazine, including an account of his VA treatment for Multiple Myeloma, related to the Agent Orange he was exposed to in the water at Long Binh, where he served in Viet Nam.

ACKNOWLEDGMENTS

First, I acknowledge my editor, Susan O'Neill. She's done all the things necessary to produce a book, things I couldn't do. Next, I acknowledge my many relatives who appear in these stories.

Aunt Nellie Mae

Aunt Aleda

My mother and father and sister

Grandpa Homer Willson

Grandpa Hulver Aspen

Grandma Kathy Willson

Grandma Alma Aspen

Thanks to the above for the stories you gave me to tell. There'd be no book without them.

Thanks to my dear friends who have encouraged me to write these stories. I intended to write down all the names, but the list got too long. I'm honored by your friendship.

Thanks to my Angel of Mercy, my wife, Michele, for keeping me alive to be able to write and to live my life. Thanks to our children who give me reason to live—Alice and Joaquin.

Thanks to our canine companions—Arlo and Woodrow. Their antics drive me nuts but keep me sane.